Narrative therapy classics

by Michael White

Dulwich Centre Publications

ADELAIDE, SOUTH AUSTRALIA

ISBN 0 9752180 8 5

Copyright © 2016 by
DULWICH CENTRE PTY LTD
Hutt St PO Box 7192
Adelaide, South Australia, 5000
dulwich @dulwichcentre.com.au
www.dulwichcentre.com.au

Preface

Preface

by Carolyn Markey

As this book was being compiled, Cheryl White invited a number of narrative therapists from different parts of the world to suggest four or five of Michael White's articles that we find particularly inspiring in supporting the work we do with families and young people. I have been fortunate enough to be using narrative ideas here in Adelaide in an ever-evolving way since I trained at Dulwich Centre, twenty-five years ago.

As a way to introduce the chapters presented in this book, I found myself thinking about the working day that I'd just had when I received Cheryl's invitation. What were the most influential narrative ideas that had supported me to navigate a path through that day? Where did the questions I found myself formulating come from? What supported me to notice whose voice, or which ideas, or discourses, had more space in each conversation? As I talk with people about their struggles and tribulations, which writings particularly challenge me to be vigilant in noticing the politics of everyday life?

On that day, I had worked as a school counsellor. I'd opened my inbox to read an email which informed me that a student's father had been missing and that there had been a major police search – a traumatic and unexpected event. I thought about how these words in my inbox could lead me to make assumptions about this young man, his father and their family – how these words unintentionally reflected thin conclusions, and how my narratively informed task was to seek richer, multi-storied accounts. Sitting in front of my computer, reading the initial referral, I knew what would be most relevant were the meanings this young man might be making about recent events.

In line with a well-intended dominant discourse of 'child in need of professional help', I'd been requested to meet with this student as soon as possible. Rather than rushing forward, however, I paused. Michael's writings, which were always informed by the knowledge of the children and families he had consulted as well as other bodies of knowledge, had me consider how the intervention of the school counsellor positioned as 'expert' may not necessarily be the most effective representation of 'help' at this time. The ways in which Michael drew upon Michael Foucault's analysis of modern power in the Western world in order to make visible the politics of therapy (See Chapter 1, 'Deconstruction and therapy'), often lead me to ask, 'How can I be vigilant to ensure that my intervention as professional expert doesn't subordinate the know-how that this family (or community) is bringing, or could bring, to respond to this crisis?'

When I did ring the family, I learnt that there had been helpful and unfamiliar interventions during the previous 48 hours which included interactions with police, hospital systems, and the media. Foremost in my mind was how my contact could be informed by an ethic of collaboration with the family and other help providers (see Chapter 7, 'Fostering collaboration').

During the initial phone call, I was also supported by Michael's determination to always enquire beyond the half-story of 'what the trauma had done to them', in order to also identify how the child and their adult care-givers had *responded* to these unfamiliar events (see Chapter 5, 'Children, trauma and subordinate storyline development'). I was interested to know what the family members, and/or their friends, were doing for each other at this time. I learnt that this young man's cherished dad had just been found, so I also enquired about this young person's thoughts about what was being helpful for his dad, for his family, and for himself at this time.

When I did meet with the student in person, the predominant theme was not 'what I can do for you?' Instead, I was equipped with a particular intent:

- to authenticate the choices he had been making in relation to how to respond to this crisis,

- to invoke and recruit supportive audiences, and

- to minimise the potential for those he loved and cherished to be pathologised.

Early on in our conversation, I asked, 'Who else knows what's been happening? Did you have a say in them knowing? What had you deciding to let certain friends know?'

These questions enabled this young man to share with me who were some of the significant members of his 'club of life' (see Chapter 3, 'Saying hullo again: The incorporation of the lost relationship in the resolution of grief' and Chapter 4, 'Re-membering'). These were the people with whom he had shared recent events. This was vital in starting to build a safe, familiar, and also fun foundation to our collaboration. After our conversation had evoked in the room the presence of supportive people – including his dad, other close friends and family, and particularly his beloved dog – I tentatively invited him to look at the words written in documents pinned on the walls of my office. These documents have been written by other students and describe ways in which they have got through hard and unfamiliar times.

A particular poem about sadness caught his attention – the first line being 'sadness is good …' We haven't spoken too much about that poem yet, but it clearly resonated with some experiences he was having. This way of sharing potential solution-knowledges *between* students links to writings about decentering the therapist, the imperative of witnesses, and bottom-up accountability (see Chapter 8, 'On ethics and spiritualities of the surface').

Michael White's groundbreaking amalgamation of philosophical, linguistic, anthropological, and feminist ideas urges us to provide every person we meet in therapy with a context that will bring forward their present but not-yet-realised insider-knowledges and skills. In my initial conversation with this young man, I sought to highlight other responses/ decisions that he and his family had made through questions like, 'How is "keeping things quiet" important for you and your dad at this time?'

In a more recent consultation with this student, he told me that his dad was now 'getting better and being safe at home'. When I asked him more about this, he initially attributed all the changes to his father's response to new medications, as this was the explanation that had been given by the father's psychiatrist. As a means to give more acknowledgement to the efforts of his father, of other family members, and to local knowledge, I asked this young man the sort of question that I know Michael White used to ask people in Glenside Psychiatric Hospital when he worked there early in his career: 'As you watch your dad at home, what do you see your dad doing now that is helping the medication to work even better?' (see Chapter 2, 'Psychotic experience and discourse').

Unexpectedly, his eyes lit up and he answered straight away with a smile, 'He's going for runs again – more than he was before – and he's going with an old friend from university. It's like he's getting back to normal!'

Next time we meet, I will ask this young man what it might mean to his dad that his son is noticing and acknowledging the dedicated efforts he is making to get his life back. I can't wait!

Every day that I work as a therapist, I rely on the ideas that are to be found in the pages of this book.

I hope, as you find time to read or re-read this beautiful collection, that the ideas and stories provide a kind of cherished company for you in the vital and complex work that you do.

About this book

Gathered here in one book are a series of papers and interviews by Michael White that transformed conventional notions of therapy, reshaped understandings of psychosis, provided new ways of responding to grief, and that continue to profoundly challenge the hegemony of psychiatric knowledges. Simultaneously moving and inspiring, these chapters convey a rare combination of political analysis and compassion.

For some, reading this book will be like sitting once again with an old friend and being re-invigorated by their company. For others, each chapter will provide unexpected challenges and possibilities. Whether you are responding to people experiencing grief, mental health struggles, or traumatic experience; whether you are meeting with children, or adults, or working with families; the stories included here and the rigour of the thinking will provide new options for practice and understanding.

Chapter one

Deconstruction and therapy

One of the classic narrative therapy texts, this chapter begins with engaging stories of practice and then provides a rigorous and thought-provoking guide for a form of therapy as deconstruction. Incidentally, the endnotes to this chapter contain descriptions of 'Escape from secrecy meetings' that are not to be missed!

This chapter was first published in the 1991 *Dulwich Centre Newsletter*, (3) 21-40. Parts of this paper were presented at the End of Grand Designs conference in Heidelberg, April 1991, and at the Generating Possibilities Through Therapeutic Conversations Conference in Tulsa, Oklahoma in July 1991. It was reprinted in Epston, D. & White, M. (1992). *Experience, contradiction, narrative & imagination*, pp. 109-152. Adelaide, Australia: Dulwich Centre Publications.

Chapter two

Psychotic experience and discourse:
An interview of Michael White by Ken Stewart

This wide-ranging interview is the place where Michael discusses in most detail the thinking that informed his work with psychotic experience. It conveys with clarity his positions on the use of psychiatric diagnoses and medication, and includes subversive challenges to the hegemony of psychiatric knowledges. At the same time, this interview also provides practical lines of enquiry for conversations with those hearing voices, creative forms of documentation, and even the inclusion of invisible friends in therapy.

This interview was first published in the book *Re-authoring lives: Interviews and essays* by Michael White (Dulwich Centre Publications, 1995). It is, in a sense, an interview within an interview. Some of the questions within it are based on an earlier interview that was conducted in 1990, but was never completed. Ken Stewart is from the Family Treatment Program at Human Services, Inc., Washington County, Minnesota, and is adjunct faculty at the Minnesota School for Professional Psychology.

Chapter three

Saying hullo again: The incorporation of the lost relationship in the resolution of grief

This text heralded a breakthrough in ways of responding to people experiencing profound and extended grief and introduced the 'Saying hullo again' metaphor to the field.

First published in the Spring 1988 issue of the *Dulwich Centre Newsletter*, this paper was prepared for the Loss and the Family International Colloquium, Ballymaloe, County Cork, Ireland, 5-8 July 1988. When first published, Michael thanked Karl Tomm for his comments on an earlier draft of this paper.

Chapter four

Re-membering

Containing a moving extended transcript of a 'saying hullo again' narrative therapy consultation, this chapter illuminates what are now known as re-membering practices. It also honours the contributions of stuffed team members, who played a significant role in much of Michael's work.

This chapter is an extract from the book *Narratives of therapists' lives* by Michael White (Dulwich Centre Publications, 1997).

Chapter five

Children, trauma and subordinate storyline development

This influential chapter emphasises the importance of subordinate storyline development in consultations with children who have been subject to trauma. This subordinate storyline development provides an alternative territory of identity for children to stand in as they begin to give voice to their experiences of trauma. This affords children a significant degree of immunity from the potential for re-traumatisation. Discussion of the use of 'the absent but implicit' is also included here.

This chapter was first published in the *International Journal of Narrative Therapy and Community Work*, 2005 (3&4), 10–21.

Chapter six

Narrative practice and the unpacking of identity conclusions

Alternating between rich stories of practice and sparkling historical and theoretical explorations, this chapter offers ways for practitioners to escape dead-ended naturalistic accounts of identity and instead fashion rich storylines of identity and engage with the unexpected. A classic read!

This chapter was first published in 2001 in *Gecko: A Journal of Deconstruction and Narrative Ideas in Therapeutic Practice*, (1), 28–55. Republished 2004 in M. White, *Narrative practice & exotic lives: Resurrecting diversity in everyday life* (Dulwich Centre Publications).

Chapter seven

Fostering collaboration – between parents and children, and between child protection services and families

This interview of Michael White by David Denborough provides valuable concepts and practical ideas for therapists working with families in which there is conflict between children or adolescents and their parents. It introduces the concept of 'positive implication' to the field of narrative practice and provides new possibilities for collaborative 'child protection' practice.

This chapter was first published in the book *Narrative therapy with children and their families* by Michael White and Alice Morgan (Dulwich Centre Publications, 2006).

Chapter eight

On ethics and spiritualities of the surface
An interview of Michael White by Michael Hoyt and Gene Combs

This interview of Michael White explores the intriguing combination of ethics and spiritualities. Ranging from references to feminist ethics, bottom-up accountability, and ways of honouring the 'sacraments of daily existence', this interview by Michael Hoyt and Gene Combs is unlike any other. It concludes with an exercise developed by Michael White highlighting the conscious purposes and commitments that therapists bring to their work.

This interview was originally published 1996 in M. F. Hoyt (Ed.), *Constructive therapies, volume 2*. New York, NY: Guilford Press. Reprinted with permission of Guilford Press. The conversation took place on 16 July 1994 at the Therapeutic Conversations 2 conference held in Reston, Virginia (near Washington, D.C.), where Michael White was serving as a core faculty member. Michael Hoyt is a California-based psychologist. He is the author/editor of numerous books, including *Some stories are better than others* (2000); *Therapist stories of inspiration, passion, and renewal: What's love got to do with it?* (2013); and *Brief therapy and beyond: Stories, language, love, hope, and time* (2017). Gene Combs is Co-director of the Evanston Family Therapy Centre (with Jill Freedman), and is co-author of *Symbol, story and ceremony* (1990) and *Narrative therapy: The social construction of preferred realities* (1996).

chapter one

Deconstruction and therapy

by Michael White

Lest some readers be disappointed, before proceeding with my discussion of deconstruction and therapy I should inform you that this paper is not about the deconstruction of the knowledges and the practices of specific and established models of therapy, or about the deconstruction of any particular therapy "movement". Rather, in this paper I have chosen to cast certain practices of therapy within the frame provided by deconstruction.

As the first and foremost concern of my professional life relates to what happens in the therapeutic context, at the outset of this paper I will present several stories of therapy. I would like to emphasize the fact that, due to space considerations, these stories are glossed. They do not adequately represent the disorderly process of therapy – the ups and downs of that adventure that we refer to as therapy. Thus, there is a simplicity reflected in these accounts that cannot be found in the work itself.

Elizabeth

Elizabeth, a sole parent[1], initially consulted me about her two daughters, aged twelve and fifteen years. She was concerned about their persistent antagonism towards her, their frequent tantrums, their abuse of her, and their apparent unhappiness. These problems had been upsetting to Elizabeth for some considerable time, and she was concerned that she might never recover from the despair that she was experiencing. She had come to the interview alone because her children refused to accompany her. As Elizabeth described these problems to me, she revealed that she had begun to experience what she thought might be "hate" for them, and this had been distressing her all the more.

When discussing with Elizabeth her concerns, I first asked about how these problems were affecting the lives of family members, and about the extent to which they were interfering in family relationships. I then asked more specifically about how these problems had been influencing her thoughts about herself: What did she believe these problems reflected about her as a parent? What conclusions had she come to about herself as a mother? Tearfully, Elizabeth confessed that she had concluded that she was a failure as a mother. With this disclosure, I began to understand something of the private story that Elizabeth had been living by.

I then inquired as to how the view that she was a failure was compelling of Elizabeth in her relationship with her children. In response to this question, she gave details of the guilt that she experienced over not having sustained a "more ideal" family environment, of her highly tenuous and apologetic interaction with her daughters, and of the extent to which she felt bound to submit herself to their evaluation of her.

Was the havoc that the view of failure, and its associated guilt, was wreaking in her life and her relationships acceptable to her? Or would Elizabeth feel more comfortable if she broke her life and her relationships free of the tyranny of this view and its associated guilt? In response to these questions, Elizabeth made it clear, in no uncertain terms, that the current status of her relationship with her children was quite untenable, and that it was time for her to intervene and have more to say about the direction of her life and the shape of this relationship.

I encouraged Elizabeth to explore how she had been recruited into this view that she was a failure as a mother and as a person, and about the mechanisms by which her guilt had been provoked. What experiences had been most instrumental in this recruitment? Did she think that women were more vulnerable to being recruited into the view that they had failed their children, or was it more likely that men would be recruited into this view? On this point she had no doubt – women!

The exploration of these questions brought forth some of the specifics of Elizabeth's recruitment into the view that she was a failure (for example, her experience as the recipient of abuse at the hands of her former husband)[2], and the wider context of the gender-specific nature of this construction (for example, the inequitable social structures that reinforce this view for sole parents who are women, and the prevalence of mother-blaming in our culture).

As we explored the various ways that the view that she was a failure had affected her life, and some of the details of how she was recruited into this view, Elizabeth began to experience in herself an identity distinct in relation to this view – failure no longer spoke to her of her identity. This development cleared the way for us to distinguish some of the areas of her life that had not been co-opted by this view.

I partly facilitated the identification of these distinctions by providing Elizabeth with an account of the myriad of ways that the idea of failure, and its associated guilt, had tyrannized the lives of other women with whom I had talked – other women who had been subject to similar processes of recruitment. I then said that it was my understanding that this sort of tyrannization was never totally effective; that it had never entirely succeeded in eclipsing the lives of these women. I gave examples: "Some of these women had escaped the effects of this view of failure in their relationships with women friends, and others had kept alive their hopes that things could be different". In response to this, Elizabeth identified instances in several areas of her life in which she had been able to resist this tyranny.

I asked Elizabeth whether she thought this resistance was a positive or negative development in her life. As she said that this was a positive development, I inquired as to why she believed this to be so. During our subsequent discussion, it was determined that these instances reflected that she had not totally submitted to these negative views of who she was, and that she had some resolve to challenge the tyranny of guilt. This provided Elizabeth with evidence that her life had not been dominated by failure.

Then, through a series of questions, I encouraged Elizabeth to trace the history of this refusal. In the process of this, she identified a couple of historical figures who had witnessed some developments in her capacity to protest certain injustices. In our subsequent discussion, Elizabeth put both of us in touch with alternative versions of who she might be, versions of herself that she clearly preferred. As these alternative and preferred versions emerged from the shadows through our discussion, they became more available to Elizabeth to enter her life into.

As Elizabeth's enthusiasm for this alternative knowledge of who she was as a person became more apparent, I discussed with her the importance of seizing the initiative in putting others in touch with what she had discovered. To this end, I encouraged her to identify persons who might provide an appropriate audience to this other version of who she might be, persons who might participate in the acknowledgement of and the authentication of this version.[3] We then discussed various ideas about how she might introduce this other version of herself to these persons, and ideas about how these persons could be invited to respond to what Elizabeth was enthusiastic about in regard to these discoveries.

As part of the exploration of other versions of who Elizabeth might be, I had asked her to identify what it was about herself that she would personally like to have in a mother. Having articulated some details of this, I suggested that it might be important to catch her children up with this. Would she be prepared to tell them what she had discovered about herself as a woman and as a mother that she could appreciate, and to continue to remind them of this from time to time? This struck a chord. Elizabeth seemed rather joyful about the idea. I was quick to share my prediction that it was unlikely that Elizabeth's efforts to "reclaim her life" would be greeted at first with great enthusiasm by her children.

Elizabeth went away determined to have more to say about who she was, and to decline her children's invitations for her to subject herself to their constant evaluation and surveillance. Initially her daughters' response to her taking over the authorship of her own life was dramatic. They came up with some very creative ideas for turning back the clock. However, Elizabeth persevered through this, and then everyone's life went forward. She forged a new connection with her daughters, they became more enthusiastic about life, the abuse subsided, and Elizabeth reported that, for the first time, they had the sort of mother-daughter relationships that she had desired. They had become more connected as confidantes, able to discuss important matters of concern with each other.

Amy

'biological'
but so many
semh
impack

Amy, aged 23 years, sought help in her struggle with anorexia nervosa. This was a longstanding problem, and it had withstood many attempts to resolve it. I first reviewed with Amy the effects that anorexia nervosa was having in the various domains of her life – including the social, the emotional, the intellectual, and, of course, the physical. In response to this review, the extent to which anorexia nervosa was making it difficult for her to make an appearance in any of these domains became apparent to both of us.

We then spent time exploring, in greater detail, how anorexia nervosa was affecting Amy's interactions with others. I wasn't surprised to learn that it had her constantly comparing herself to others, and that it had instilled in her a sense that she was being perpetually evaluated by others. Apart from this, it was enforcing a shroud of secrecy around her life, and isolating her from others.

How was the anorexia nervosa affecting Amy's attitude towards, and interaction with, herself? What was it requiring her to do to herself? Predictably, it was requiring her to watch over herself, to police herself. It had her engaging in operations on her own body, attempting to forge it into a shape that might be considered acceptable – a "docile body". And it had her punishing her own body for its transgressions.

I then engaged Amy in an investigation of how she had been recruited into these various practices, procedures and attitudes; these "disciplines of the self" according to gendered specifications for personhood; this hierarchical and disciplinary attitude and relationship to her own body. In this investigation, Amy was able to identify a history to this recruitment though familial, cultural and social contexts. In our subsequent discussion, anorexia nervosa appeared as the embodiment of these attitudes, practices and contexts.

Through this therapeutic process, anorexia nervosa was "unmasked", and Amy became increasingly alienated from it. The various taken-for-granted practices and attitudes that anorexia nervosa "relied upon for its survival" no longer spoke to her of the truth of who she was as a person. Would Amy be content to continue to submit to anorexia nervosa's claims on her life, to continue to defer to its requirements? Or was she more attracted to the idea of challenging its claims to her life, and to the idea of taking her life over and making it her own?

Amy had no hesitation in stating that it was time to make her life her own, so together we reviewed the available evidence that she might be able to do so: events that reflected resistance to the practices and attitudes upon which that state of "the government of self" called anorexia nervosa depended. This led to the identification of various developments or events that were of an anti-anorectic nature.[4]

I asked Amy to evaluate these anti-anorectic developments: did she consider these to be the more attractive and desirable developments in her life, or did she consider them trivial and unappealing? In response, Amy judged these developments to be the preferred developments in her life. I then engaged her in a conversation about why she thought these developments were desirable, and about why she thought they personally suited her.

As Amy seemed to be more strongly supporting these anti-anorectic activities, I encouraged her to help me understand the basis or the foundation of these in her life. I also encouraged her to reflect upon what these preferred developments said about what she believed was important for her life. During the ensuing discussion, Amy began to more fully articulate a preferred version of who she might be, one that incorporated alternative knowledges of life. This version gradually became available to her to enter her life into and to live by.

As Amy began to articulate and perform this alternative and preferred version of who she was, she took various steps to engage others in her project to reclaim her life. These steps were encouraged by my observation that "fieldwork" was an integral part of any such project. I had asked Amy to identify who, of all those persons who had known her, might be the least inaccessible to this new view of who she was.[5]

She decided to begin by re-introducing herself to those who were "far away", and contacted several school friends whom she had not seen for several years. Experiencing success in this, she moved to her more immediate social network, which included members of her family of origin, whom she began to invite along to the therapy session. Within the therapeutic context, these family members contributed significantly to the acknowledgement of, and the authentication of, Amy's preferred claims about her life, and to Amy's ability to separate her life from anorexia nervosa.

Anne and John

John and Anne, a separating couple, sought therapy in an attempt to resolve their intense conflict over custody and access in relation to their children, and over property settlement. At the outset of the first meeting, they entered into a fierce dispute, each presenting various claims and counter claims, and only occasionally glancing furtively in my direction. After a time, I interrupted, thanking them both for being so open about the problems they were having with each other, and for providing such a clear demonstration of how things go for them.

After a pause, John and Anne launched into a fresh round of accusations. Fortunately, I was again able to interrupt, explaining that I believed I had a reasonable understanding of their experience of the relationship, and informing them that further demonstrations of this would be unnecessary. Two further such interruptions were necessary before the couple seemed convinced of this.

In the breathing space that followed, I asked to what extent this pattern of interacting – the adversarial one that they had just so clearly demonstrated – was dominating of their relationship; How was this adversarial pattern influencing their perceptions of each other and of their relationship? And how were these perceptions of each other and of their relationship influencing their responses to each other? What did this adversarial pattern have them doing to each other that might be against their better judgement?

After reviewing, with Anne and John, the extent to which this adversarial pattern had been dictating the terms of their relationship, I asked them if this had become their preferred way of responding to each other. Did they find this adversarial pattern captivating? Did this way of being with each other suit them best? Was this adversarial pattern of relating to each other tailor-made for them? Did they experience this way of being together as enriching of their lives?

Both claimed that this was not their preferred way of relating to the other, and both couldn't resist adding that it did seem the preference of the other partner. Since John and Anne claimed that this was not their preferred way of going about things, I suggested that it was unlikely that they had invented it for themselves.

I then encouraged Anne and John to help me understand how they had been recruited into this pattern of responding to differences of opinion over particular issues, and to identify the history of this pattern. Where had they witnessed this pattern before? How were they originally introduced to these techniques for dealing with each other, and what situations first exposed them to these techniques? In what contexts would they expect to find these patterns commonplace, and what justifications are referred to most frequently in order to sustain them? How were they encouraged to subject their relationship to these patterns, to live their relationship out through these patterns?

During this discussion, as John and Anne articulated their experience of this adversarial pattern, it became apparent to them that their relationship was no longer at one with this pattern – they were able to think otherwise about their relationship. I asked them if they were prepared to leave what was left of their relationship to the designs of these patterns, or if they would prefer to intervene and have more to say about the direction of events – to determine a design for what was left of their relationship that would suit them both? In response to this question, John and Anne said that the adversarial pattern was impoverishing their lives, and both indicated that they wanted to free themselves from its dictates.

We then worked to determine what basis there was for an attempt to retrieve what was left of their relationship, and managed to identify several interactions that had not been dominated by the adversarial pattern. One of these related to the extent to which they had been able to evade this pattern for a good part of the interview. Did Anne and John find these interactions with each other more satisfying? Were they at all enthusiastic about these developments? Or were they more attracted to their more familiar ways of being with each other?

As they determined that they were more attracted to this alternative way of interacting with each other, I asked John and Anne what they thought this way of being together had going for it, and why they thought it would suit them to extend these developments. Following this I introduced questions that encouraged them to historicize these more positive developments in their relationship. In responding to these questions, Anne and John recalled a couple that they had befriended early in their marriage. This couple had witnessed several occasions upon which they had been able to resolve a dispute satisfactorily and equitably. A review of this other couple's experience of John and Anne's relationship led to the resurrection of historically situated problem solving knowledges, and, although not without hitches, these became available to them to resolve their disputes over custody, access and property.

Robert

Robert was referred for therapy over abusive behaviour in relation to his partner, and in relation to one of his children. This abuse had only been recently disclosed. He had agreed to leave the family home, and the appropriate police and court measures were in the process of being instituted.

During our early contact, discussion centred on Robert's responsibility for perpetrating the abuse[6], on the identification of the survivors' experiences of abuse, on the real short-term and possible long-term traumatic effects of this on the life of the survivors, and on determining what he might do to take responsibility to mend what might be mended.

Following this work, I asked Robert whether he would be prepared to join me in some speculation about the conditions and the character of men's abusive behaviour. This he agreed to do, so I asked him a series of questions within the category of those represented below:

- *If a man wanted to control and to dominate another person, what sort of structures and conditions could he arrange that would make this possible?*

- *If a man desired to dominate another person, particularly a woman or a child, what sort of attitudes would be necessary in order to justify this?*

- *If a man decided to make someone their captive, particularly a woman or a child, what sort of strategies and techniques of power would make this feasible?*

During this speculation, particular knowledges about men's ways of being that are subjugating of others were articulated, techniques and strategies that men could rely upon to institute this subjugation were identified, and various structures and conditions that support abusive behaviour were reviewed. I then asked Robert to determine which of these attitudes he had given his life to, which of these strategies had been dominant in shaping his relationships with others, and which of these conditions and structures had provided the framework for his life. This was followed by further discussion centred on a review of the historical processes through which Robert had been recruited into the life space that was fabricated of these attitudes, techniques and structures.

Robert was invited to take a position on these attitudes, strategies and structures. Would he continue to subject his life to this particular knowledge of men's way of being? To what extent did he think it was reasonable to live life as "power's instrument", as an instrument of terror? To what extent did he wish to co-operate with these strategies and tactics that so devastated the lives of others? In view of his developing understanding of the real effects of his actions, did he think it acceptable to depend upon these structures and conditions as a framework for his life?

As this work progressed, Robert began to experience a separation from these attitudes, and an alienation from these structures and techniques of power and control. His previously familiar and taken-for-granted ways of being in relation to women and children, and for that matter, his previously familiar and taken-for-granted ways of being with other men, no longer spoke to him of the truth of who he was as a man. For Robert to challenge his abusive behaviour no longer meant taking action against his own "nature", and he was now able to take entire responsibility for the abuse that he had perpetrated on others.

In the space that Robert stepped into as a result of this separation, we were able to find various unique outcomes; occasions upon which his behaviour had not been compelled by those previously familiar and taken-for-granted ways of being as a man. I asked Robert to evaluate these unique outcomes – did he see these outcomes as desirable? Did he feel positively about them? Or were they of no consequence to him? As Robert concluded that these outcomes were desirable, I asked him to share with me how he had reached this conclusion.

As our work progressed, the identification of these unique outcomes provided a point of entry for an "archeology" of alternative and preferred knowledges of men's ways of being, knowledges that Robert began to enter his life into. For example, in response to my encouragement to give meaning to these unique outcomes, to determine what ways of "being" as a man were reflected in them, Robert recalled an uncle who was quite unlike other men in his family; this was a man who was certainly compassionate and non-abusive. Robert subsequently did some homework on this uncle, and this contributed significantly to his knowledge of some of the more intimate particularities of this alternative way of being.

Robert's family had signalled a strong desire to explore the possibilities of reuniting[7]. As Robert had begun to separate from those attitudes and practices that had justified and supported his abusive behaviour, and as he had entered into an exploration of alternative and preferred knowledges of men's ways of being, the time seemed right to convene a meeting with the family.[8] Understanding his responsibility to provide safeguards to family members, he agreed to participate in certain structures that would contribute significantly to the security of family members. These included (a) a meeting with representatives[9] of his partner and his child to disclose his responsibility for and the nature of the abuse, (b) weekly escape from secrecy meetings[10,11] with his family and the nominated representatives, and (c) co-operation with other family members in the development of a contingency plan should any family member again feet threatened by abuse.

Over time, Robert traded a neglectful and strategic life for one that he, and others, considered to be caring, open and direct.

An interview with a family

The interview had reached a point at which the therapist decided that it was time to hear from the team members who had been observing the interview from behind a one-way screen. The therapist and the family traded places with the team members; it was now their turn to be an audience to the team members' reflections. The team members first introduced themselves to the family. They then proceeded to share their responses to what family members had judged, or had seemed attracted to, as preferred developments in their lives and relationships.

It was the team members' task to relate to these preferred developments as one might relate to a mystery, a mystery that only family members could unravel. Initially, each observation from a team member was followed by questions that might encourage family members to account for these developments, and questions that might engage them in speculation about what these developments might mean. Team members also addressed questions to each other about these developments, inviting further speculation about them. In this way, the family members' fascination in relation to previously neglected aspects of their lived experience was engaged, and they were provoked to enlist their "knowledgeableness" in regard to their own lives.

Some team members then began to ask other team members about why they found a particular development interesting. These questions encouraged team members to situate their reflections within the context of their personal experience and their imagination. Team members then invited each other to make transparent what they understood to be the intentions behind their reflections.

Following this, the family and the team again traded places, and the therapist proceeded to interview family members about their experience of the team's reflections; about what comments and questions family members found to be of interest and to the point, and about what comments and questions were not so. As family members began to relate those comments and questions that caught their interest, the therapist asked them to help her understand why they found these interesting, and what realizations and/or conclusions accompanied these comments and questions. The therapist then encouraged family members' speculative assessment about how these realizations and conclusions could affect their day-to-day lives.

The therapist brought the interview to a close by inviting family members and the reflecting team to interview her about the interview, so that she might situate her comments and questions within the context of her own personal experience, imagination and purposes.

Deconstruction

These stories about therapy portray a number of recurrent practices. I believe that most of these practices relate to what could be referred to as a "deconstructive method", which will be explicated in the following discussion.

I should preface this discussion of deconstruction with an admission – I am not an academic, but, for the want of a better word, a therapist. It is my view that not being situated in the academic world allows me certain liberties, including the freedom to break some rules – for example, to use the term deconstruction in a way that may not be in accord with its strict Derridian sense – and to refer to writers who may not generally be considered to be proposing a deconstructivist method.

According to my rather loose definition, deconstruction has to do with procedures that subvert taken-for-granted realities and practices; those so-called "truths" that are split off from the conditions and the context of their production, those disembodied ways of speaking that hide their biases and prejudices, and those familiar practices of self and of relationship that are subjugating of persons' lives. Many of the methods of deconstruction render strange these familiar and everyday taken-for-granted realities and practices by objectifying them. In this sense, the methods of deconstruction are methods that "exoticize the domestic":

> The sociologist who chooses to study his [sic] own world in its nearest and most familiar aspects should not, as the ethnologist would domesticate the exotic, but, if I may venture the expression, exoticize the domestic, through a break with his [sic] initial relation of intimacy with modes of life and thought which remain opaque to him [sic] because they are too familiar. In fact the movement towards the originary, and the ordinary, world should be the culmination of a movement toward alien and extraordinary worlds. (Bourdieu, 1988, pp. xi–xii)

23

According to Bourdieu, exoticizing the domestic through the objectification of a familiar and taken-for-granted world facilitates the "reappropriation" of the self. In referring to the reappropriation of the self, I do not believe that he is proposing an essentialist view of self – that in this re-appropriation persons will "find" themselves. Rather, he is suggesting that through the objectification of a familiar world, we might become more aware of the extent to which certain "modes of life and thought" shape our existence, and that we might then be in a position to choose to live by other "modes of life and thought".

If Bourdieu's work can be considered deconstructive, then it is so in a specific sense. His primary interest is in the extent to which a person's situation in a social structure – for example, in academia – is constituting of that person's stance on issues in life

However, we can also consider deconstruction in other senses: for example, the deconstruction of self-narrative and the dominant cultural knowledges that persons live by; the deconstruction of practices of self and of relationship that are dominantly cultural; and the deconstruction of the discursive practices of our culture.

Deconstruction is premised on what is generally referred to as a "critical constructivist", or, as I would prefer, a "constitutionalist" perspective on the world. From this perspective, it is proposed that persons' lives are shaped by the meaning that they ascribe to their experience, by their situation in social structures, and by the language practices and cultural practices of self and of relationship that these lives are recruited into. This constitutionalist perspective is at variance with the dominant structuralist (behaviour reflects the structure of the mind) and functionalist (behaviour serves a purpose for the system) perspectives of the world of psychotherapy.

In the following discussion, I will consider first the deconstruction of narrative, second, the deconstruction of modern practices of power, and third, the deconstruction of discursive practices. However, I believe, with Michel Foucault (1980), that a domain of knowledge is a domain of power, and that a domain of power is a domain of knowledge. Thus, inasmuch as meaning relates to knowledge, and inasmuch as practices relate to power, I believe that meaning, structures and practices are inseparable in their constitutive aspects.

24

Meaning

The idea that it is the meaning which persons attribute to their experience that is constitutive of those persons' lives has encouraged social scientists to explore the nature of the frames that facilitate the interpretation of experience. Many of these social scientists have proposed that it is the narrative or story that provides the primary frame for this interpretation, for the activity of meaning-making; that it is through the narratives or the stories that persons have about their own lives and the lives of others that they make sense of their experience. Not only do these stories determine the meaning that persons give to experience, it is argued, but these stories also largely determine which aspects of experience persons select out for expression. And, as well, inasmuch as action is prefigured on meaning-making, these stories determine real effects in terms of the shaping of persons' lives.

This perspective should not be confused with that which proposes that stories function as a reflection of life or as a mirror for life. Instead, the narrative metaphor proposes that persons live their lives by stories – that these stories are shaping of life, and that they have real, not imagined, effects – and that these stories provide the structure of life.

In the family therapy literature there are many examples of the conflating of the narrative metaphor and of various conversation/linguistic metaphors. As these metaphors are situated in distinctly different traditions of thought, and as some are at variance with others, I will here present some further thoughts about the narrative metaphor that I hope will adequately distinguish it.

Narrative structure

Bruner (1986), in referring to texts, proposed that stories are composed of dual landscapes – a "landscape of action and a "landscape of consciousness". The landscape of action is constituted of (a) events that are linked together in (b) particular sequences through the (c) temporal dimension – through past, present and future – and according to (d) specific plots. In a text, the landscape of action provides the reader with a perspective on the thematic unfolding of events across time.

The landscape of consciousness is significantly constituted by the interpretations of the characters in the story, and also by those of the reader as s/he enters, at the invitation of the writer, the consciousness of these characters. The landscape of consciousness features the meanings derived by characters and readers through "reflection" on the events and plots as they unfold through the landscape of action. Perceptions, thoughts, speculation, realizations and conclusions dominate this landscape, and many of these relate to:

(a)   the determination of the desires and the preferences of the characters,

(b)   the identification of their personal and relationship characteristics and qualities,

(c)   the clarification of their intentional states – for example, their motives and their purposes – and, to

(d)   the substantiation of the beliefs of these characters.

As these desires, qualities, intentional states and beliefs become sufficiently elaborated through the text, they coalesce into "commitments" that determine particular careers in life – "life-styles".

If we assume that there is an identity between the structure of texts and the structure of the stories or narratives that persons live by, and if we take as our interest the constitution of lives through stories, we might then consider the details of how persons live their lives through landscapes of action and landscapes of consciousness.

Determinacy

What is the origin of these stories or narratives that are constitutive of persons' lives? The stories that persons live by are rarely, if ever, "radically" constructed – it is not a matter of them being made-up, "out of the blue", so to speak. Our culturally available and appropriate stories about personhood and about relationship have been historically constructed and negotiated in communities of persons, and within the context of social structures and institutions. Inevitably, there is a canonical dimension to the stories that persons live by.

Thus, these stories are inevitably framed by our dominant cultural knowledges. These knowledges are not about discoveries regarding the "nature" of persons and of relationships, but are constructed knowledges that are specifying of a particular strain of personhood and of relationship. For example, in regard to dominant knowledges of personhood, in the West these establish a highly individual and gender distinct specification for ways of being in the world.

Indeterminacy within determinacy

If it is the case that the stories that persons have about their lives circumscribe the meanings that they give to experience, as well as the aspects of experience that they select out for expression, and if it is the case that these meanings have particular and real effects in persons' lives, then we have a strong argument for determinacy. And this argument for determinacy is strengthened upon consideration of the extent to which such stories are canonical in that they are co-authored within a community of persons, and in that they are historically constructed within the context of specific institutions and social structures.

However, despite the fact that these stories contribute a certain determinacy to life, rarely do they handle all of the contingencies that arise in "life as lived" in anything like an accomplished way. Just as with texts, in reference to life as lived, the stories that persons live by are full of gaps and inconsistencies, and, as well, these stories constantly run up against contradictions. It is the resolution of these gaps, inconsistencies, and contradictions that contributes to a certain indeterminacy of life; it is these gaps, inconsistencies, and contradictions that provoke persons to engage actively in the performance of unique meaning, or, as Bruner (1990) would have it, in "meaning-making".

Thus, when considering the proposition that life is constituted through an ongoing storying and re-storying of experience, we are considering a process of "indeterminacy within determinacy" – or to what Gertz (1986) concludes to be a "copying that originates":

The wrenching question, sour and disabused, that Lionel Trilling somewhere quotes an eighteenth-century aesthetician as asking – "How Comes It that we all start out Originals and end up Copies?" – finds ... an answer that is surprisingly reassuring: it is the copying that originates. (p. 380)

The deconstruction of narrative

Externalizing conversations

For the deconstruction of the stories that persons live by, I have proposed the objectification of the problems for which persons seek therapy (for example, White, 1984, 1986, 1989; White & Epston, 1989). This objectification engages persons in externalizing conversations in relation to that which they find problematic, rather than internalizing conversations. This externalizing conversation generates what might be called a counter-language, or as David Epston has recently proposed, an "anti-language".

These externalizing conversations "exoticize the domestic" in that they encourage persons to identify the private stories and the cultural knowledges that they live by; those stories and knowledges that guide their lives and that speak to them of their identity. These externalizing conversations assist persons to unravel, across time, the constitution of their self and of their relationships. Externalizing conversations are initiated by encouraging persons to provide an account of the effects of the problem on their lives. This can include its effects on their emotional states, familial and peer relationships, social and work spheres etc, and with a special emphasis on how it has affected their "view" of themselves and of their relationships. Then, persons are invited to map the influence that these views or perceptions have on their lives, including on their interactions with others. This is often followed by some investigation of how persons have been recruited into these views.

As persons become engaged in these externalizing conversations, their private stories cease to speak to them of their identity and of the truth of their relationships – these private stories are no longer transfixing of their lives. Persons experience a separation from, and an alienation in relation to, these stories. In the space established by this separation, persons are free to explore alternative and preferred knowledges of who they might be; alternative and preferred knowledges into which they might enter their lives.

Unique outcomes and alternative stories

How are these alternative knowledges generated and/or resurrected? What are the points of entry to these other versions of who persons might be? As persons separate from the dominant or "totalizing" stories that are constitutive of their lives, it becomes more possible for them to orient themselves to aspects of their experience that contradict these knowledges. Such contradictions are ever present, and, as well, they are many and varied. Previously, following Goffman, I have referred to these contradictions as "unique outcomes" (White, 1988a, 1989; White & Epston, 1989), and it is these that provide a gateway to what we might consider to be the alternative territories of a person's life.

For an event to comprise a unique outcome, it must be qualified as such by the persons to whose life the event relates. Following the identification of events that are candidates for a unique outcome status, it is important that persons be invited to evaluate these events; are these events judged to be significant, or to be irrelevant? Do these events represent preferred outcomes, or do they not? Do persons find these developments appealing? Are persons attracted to some of the new possibilities that might accompany these events? If these events are judged to represent preferred outcomes, then persons can be encouraged to give an account of why they believe this to be the case.

When it is established that particular events qualify as unique outcomes in that they are judged to be both significant and preferred, the therapist can facilitate the generation of and/or resurrection of alternative stories by orienting him/herself to these unique outcomes as one might orient themselves to mysteries. These are mysteries that only persons can unravel as they respond to the therapist's curiosity about them. As persons take up the task of unravelling such mysteries, they immediately engage in story-telling and meaning-making.

To facilitate this process which I have called "re-authoring", the therapist can ask a variety of questions, including those that might be referred to as "landscape of action" questions and "landscape of consciousness" questions[12]. Landscape of action questions encourage persons to situate unique outcomes in sequences of events that unfold across time according to particular plots. Landscape of consciousness questions encourage persons to reflect on and to determine the meaning of those developments that occur in the landscape of action.

Landscape of action questions

Landscape of action questions can be referenced to the past, present and future, and are effective in bringing forth alternative landscapes that stretch through these temporal domains. In the following discussion, due to considerations of space, I will focus mainly on those questions that resurrect and generate alternative historical landscapes; questions that are historicizing of "unique outcomes". However, some future oriented landscape of action questions will feature in some of the examples that I give.

Questions that historicize unique outcomes are particularly effective in bringing forth alternative landscapes of action. These questions bridge those preferred developments of the present with the past; they encourage persons to identify the history of unique outcomes by locating them within particular sequences of events that unfold through time. Often, these questions assist persons to plot the history of the alternative landscape of action to the extent that they reach back and predate the landscapes of action of the previously dominant and "problem-saturated" stories that persons have had about their lives.

Landscape of action questions can focus on both the recent history and the more distant history of unique outcomes. Those landscape of action questions that bring forth the recent history of the unique outcome mostly relate to its more immediate circumstances:

- *How did you get yourself ready to take this step? What preparations led up to it?*

- *Just prior to taking this step, did you nearly turn back? If so, how did you stop yourself from doing so?*

- *Looking back from this vantage point, what did you notice yourself doing that might have contributed to this achievement?*

- *Could you give me some background to this? What were the circumstances surrounding this achievement? Did anyone else make a contribution? If so, would you describe this?*

- *What were you thinking at the time? Have you been advising yourself differently? What did you tell yourself that pulled you through on this occasion?*
- *What developments have occurred in other areas of your life that may relate to this? How do you think these developments prepared the way for you to take these steps?*

The therapist can encourage the participation of other persons in this generation/resurrection of alternative and preferred landscapes of action. Including members of the community of persons who have participated historically in the negotiation of, and distribution of, the dominant story of the person's life is particularly helpful. For example, other family members can make particularly significant and authenticating contributions to these alternative landscapes of action:

- *How do you think your parents managed to keep their act together in the face of this crisis?*
- *What have you witnessed Harry doing recently that could throw some light on how he was able to take this step?*
- *What did you see Sally doing leading up to this achievement? How does this contribute to an understanding of how she got ready for it?*
- *Would you describe to me the circumstances surrounding this development in your son's life? Did anyone else contribute to this, and if so, in what way?*

The following questions provide examples of those that bring forth the more distant history of the unique outcome. These invite the identification of events and experiences that have a less immediate relation to the unique outcomes. As with those questions that bring forth the recent history of the unique outcome, it is helpful to engage, as co-authors, members of the community of persons who contributed historically to the negotiation and distribution of the dominant story that is repudiated in this re-authoring process.

- *What can you tell me about your history that would help me to understand how you managed to take this step?*

- *Are you aware of any past achievements that might, in some way, provide the back-drop for this recent development?*

- *What have you witnessed in your life up to now that could have given you at least some hint that this was a possibility for you?*

- *I would like to get a better grasp of this development. What did you notice yourself doing or thinking as a younger person, that could have provided some vital clue that this development was on the horizon of your life? Please think about your son's recent feat and reflect on his life as you have known it. With hindsight, what do you recall him doing that could have foreshadowed this, that could have given you a lead on this?*

- *It seems that what Mary and Joe have recently accomplished is a manifestation of some behind the scenes work that they have been doing to retrieve their relationship. Were you aware of any signs that this work was taking place? If so, what were these signs?*

These examples provide just some of the options for engaging persons in the generation/resurrection of alternative landscapes of action, and I believe that it is not possible to exhaust the choices for this sort of interaction with persons. For example, questions can be introduced to encourage persons to bring forth the recent history and distant history of those events in history that have foreshadowed the current unique outcomes.

As persons begin to articulate preferred events in these alternative landscapes of action, and as they become more engaged in the arrangement or linking of these events in particular sequences through time, they can be encouraged to explicitly name the alternative plot or the counter-plot that is suggested by this arrangement. The name of the alternative plot or counter-plot is important, for it, among other things, (a) contributes very significantly to a person's sense of their life going forward in preferred ways, (b) makes possible the attribution of meaning to events or experiences that would otherwise be neglected or considered to be of little significance, (c) facilitates the session by session sorting and linking of the events that have taken place between sessions, and (d) provides for persons a sense of knowing what might be the next step in their preferred direction in life.

The alternative plot or counter-plot is often named quite spontaneously in the process of this work. When it is not, the therapist can facilitate this by asking questions that encourage persons to generate descriptions in juxtaposition to the previously dominant plot. Through these questions, persons who have been concerned about "losing their relationship" (previously dominant plot), may determine that these developments in the alternative landscape of action suggest that they are on the path of "reclaiming their relationship" (alternative plot or counter-plot). A person who concludes that "self-neglect" has been highly influential in their life (previously dominant plot), may decide that the developments in the alternative landscape of action reflect that s/he has been engaged in a "self-nurturing project" (alternative plot or counter-plot).

Landscape of consciousness questions

Landscape of consciousness questions encourage persons to review the developments as they unfold through the alternative landscape of action[13], and to determine what these might reveal about:

(a)   the nature of their preferences and their desires,

(b)   the character of various personal and relationship qualities,

(c)   the constitution of their intentional states,

(d)   the composition of their preferred beliefs, and, lastly,

(c)   the nature of their commitments.

Landscape of consciousness questions encourage the articulation and the performance of these alternative preferences, desires, personal and relationship qualities, and intentional states and beliefs, and this culminates in a "re-vision" of personal commitment in life.[14] It is through the performance of meaning in the landscape of consciousness that: "... peoples' beliefs and desires become sufficiently coherent and well organized as to merit being called 'commitments' or 'ways of life' and such coherences are seen as 'dispositions' that characterize persons' (Bruner, 1990, p. 39).

The following questions provide an example of just some of the forms that landscape of consciousness questions might take. These invite persons to reflect on developments as they have unfolded in both the recent and the more distant history of the landscape of action.

- *Let's reflect for a moment on these recent developments. What new conclusions might you reach about your tastes; about what is appealing to you; about what you are attracted to?*
- *What do these discoveries tell you about what you want for your life?*
- *I understand that you are more aware of the background to this turning point in Mary's life. How does this effect the picture that you have of her as a person?*
- *How would you describe the qualities that you experienced in your relationship at this earlier time, when you managed to support each other in the face of adversity?*
- *What do these developments inform you about what suits you as a person?*
- *In more fully appreciating what went into this achievement, what conclusions might you reach about what Harry intends for his life?*
- *It seems that we are both now more in touch with how you prepared yourself for this step. What does this reveal to you about your motives, or about the purposes you have for your life?*
- *What does this history of struggle suggest about what Jane believes to be important in life, about what she stands for?*

As persons respond to landscape of action and landscape of consciousness questions, they engage in a reliving of experience, and their lives are "retold". Alternative knowledges of self and of relationships are generated and/or resurrected; alternative modes of life and thought become available for persons to enter into. Throughout this re-authoring dialogue, the therapist plays a central role in challenging any early return to the canonical that would suggest that the unique outcome is self-explanatory.

Experience of experience questions

Experience of experience questions (White, 1988b) greatly facilitate the re-authoring of lives and relationships, and often they are more generative than those questions that encourage the person to reflect more directly on their life. These questions encourage persons to provide an account of what they believe or imagine to be another person's experience of them. These experience of experience questions:

(a) invite persons to reach back into their stock of lived experience and to express certain aspects that have been forgotten or neglected with the passage of time, and

(b) recruit the imagination of persons in ways that are constitutive of alternative experiences of themselves.

Some examples of these experience of experience questions follow. In the examples, these questions are oriented first to alternative landscapes of action, and second to alternative landscapes of consciousness. In the third place, examples are given of questions that encourage persons to bring forth the "intimate particularities" of future developments in these landscapes of action and landscapes of consciousness.

Of course, these questions are not asked in a barrage-like fashion. Instead, they are raised within the context of dialogue, and each is sensitively attuned to the responses triggered by the previous question.

(a) *If I had been a spectator to your life when you were a younger person, what do you think I might have witnessed you doing then that might help me to understand how you were able to achieve what you have recently achieved? What do you think this tells me about what you have wanted for your life, and about what you have been trying for in your life?*

- *How do you think that knowing this has affected my view of you as a person?*

- *What do you think this might reveal to me about what you value most?*

- *If you managed to keep this knowledge about who you are close to you over the next week or two, how would it affect the shape of your life?*

(b) *Of all those persons who have known you, who would be least surprised that you have been able to take this step in challenging the problem's influence in your life?*

- *What might they have witnessed you doing, in times past, that would have made it possible for them to predict that you could take such a step at this point in your life?[15]*

- *What do you imagine this told them, at that time, about your capabilities?*

- *What would they have assumed to be your purposes in taking this action at this point in your history? How do you think this spoke to them of who you are, and about what you believe to be important?*

- *Exactly what actions would you be committing yourself to if you were to more fully embrace this knowledge of who you are?*

(c) *I would like to understand the foundations upon which this achievement rests. Of all those persons who have known you, who would be best placed to supply some details about these foundations?*

- *What clues did this provide them with as to which developments in your life were most desirable to you?*

- *What conclusions might they have reached about your intentions in building up these foundations?*

- *What could this have disclosed to them about the sort of life-style you are more suited to?*

- *If you were to side more strongly with this other view of who you are, and of what your life has been about, what difference would this make to your life on a day-to-day basis?*

These examples serve only as an introduction to some of the options for developing questions that encourage the re-authoring of lives according to preferred stories. Among the many other options is the construction of questions that might bring forth future developments in the landscape of consciousness. These questions encourage a reflection on future events in the alternative landscape of action. For example:

- *If you did witness yourself taking these steps, how might this confirm and extend on this preferred view of who you are as a person?*

These questions can then be followed up by further landscape of action questions, and so on. For example:

- *And what difference would the confirmation of this view make to how you lived your life?*

Other structures

In the shaping of suitable questions, it can be helpful for the therapist to refer to other structures in this work, including those derived from anthropology, drama and literature. For example, at times unique outcomes appear to mark turning points for which it is difficult to find any antecedents in distant history. Under these circumstances, persons can be encouraged to plot these unique outcomes into a "rite of passage" frame that structures transitions in life through the stages of separation, liminality, and reincorporation (van Gennep, 1960).

Alternatively, under these circumstances, unique outcomes can be plotted into a "social drama" frame that structures transitions in life through the stages of steady state, breach, crisis, redress, and new steady state (Turner, 1980).

In regard to the borrowing of structures from literature, as I have discvered that the re-vision of motive that accompanies the resurrection of alternative stories and knowledges is particularly "liberating" for persons, I often refer to Burke's deconstruction of motive as a frame for this work:

> We shall use five terms as generating principle of our investigation. They are: Act, Scene, Agent, Agency, Purpose. In a rounded statement about motives, you must have some word that names the act (names what took place, in thought or deed), and another that names the scene (the background of the act the situation in which it occurred); also, you must indicate what person or kind of person (agent) performed the act, what means or instruments he [sic] used (agency), and the purpose ... any complete statement about motives will offer some kind of answer to these five questions: what was done (act), when or where it was done (scene), who did it (agent), how he [sic] did it (agency), and why (purpose). (Burke, 1969, p. xv)

In relating experience of experience questions to alternative and historically situated motives, particular acts, scenes, agents, agency, and purposes, can be brought forth.[16] This contributes "dramatically" to the archaeology of alternative knowledges of personhood and of relationship. An example of the line of questioning that is informed by this structure follows:

(a) *Okay, so your Aunt Mavis might have been best placed to predict such an achievement. Give me an example of the sort of event, that she witnessed in your life, that would have enabled her to predict this achievement.*

(b) *How might she have described the circumstances of the event?*

(c) *Would she have been aware of others who might have contributed to the event?*

(d) *If she had been asked to describe exactly how this was achieved, what do you imagine she would have said?*

(e) *What would she have construed your purposes to be in making this achievement? What do you think she might have learned about what you intended for your life?*

Discussion

At the risk of labouring the point, I want to emphasize that these landscape of action and landscape of consciousness questions are not simply questions about history. They are questions that historicize the unique outcome. And the re-authoring approach that I am describing here is not simply a process of "pointing out positives". Instead, this approach actively engages persons in unravelling mysteries that the therapist can't solve.

When I am teaching this work, following Bruner (1986), I often suggest to therapists that they envision an arch. The arch is a relatively recent development in history[17], and it owes its extraordinary load bearing performance to a specific and sequential arrangement of wedge-shaped stones. Each of these stones is uniquely placed; each stone owes its position to the particular arrangement of stones on either side of it, and in turn makes possible the particular arrangement of stones on either side of it.

difference between narrative + therapy?

38

The landscape of action can be represented as an arch. And the unique outcome can be represented as one of the wedge-shaped stones, its existence understood to be contingent upon its place in a particular class and sequence of events that unfold through time, while at the same time contributing to the particular arrangements of events, across time, on either side of it. Questions that contextualize unique outcomes contribute significantly to bringing forth details about the unique arrangement of events of which the unique outcome is but a part.

A second arch can be envisaged above the first. The landscape of consciousness can be represented by this, and it interacts back and forth with the first arch, the landscape of action, through reflection.

Perhaps the approach that I have described here on the deconstruction of the stories and knowledges that persons live by is not entirely dissimilar to Derrida's work on the deconstruction of texts (1981).[18] Derrida's intention was to subvert texts and challenge the privileging of specific knowledges with methods that "deconstruct the opposition ... to overturn the hierarchy at a given moment". He achieved this by developing deconstructive methods that:

(a) brought forth the hidden contradictions in texts, and rendering visible the repressed meanings – the "absent but implied" meanings,

(b) gave prominence to those knowledges "on the other side", those considered to be secondary, derivative and worthless.

Practices of power

A good part of Michel Foucault's work is devoted to the analysis of the "practices of power" through which the modern "subject" is constituted (Foucault, 1978, 1979). He traced the history of the "art of the government of persons" from the seventeenth century, and detailed many of the practices of self and practices of relationship that persons are incited to enter their lives into. In that it is through these practices that persons shape their lives according to dominant specifications for being, they can be considered techniques of social control.

Constitutive power

Foucault's (1980) conception was of a modern power that is constitutive or "positive" in its character and effects, not repressive or "negative"; not a power that is dependent upon prohibitions and restrictions.

Rather than propose that the central mechanism of this modern form of power was containing or restricting, he proposed that its central mechanism was productive – persons' lives are actually constituted or made up through this form of power. According to Foucault, the practices of this form of power permeate and fabricate persons' lives at the deepest levels – including their gestures, desires, bodies, habits etc. – and he likened these practices to a form of "dressage" (Foucault, 1979).

Local politics

Foucault was intent on exposing the operations of power at the micro-level and at the periphery of society: in clinics, prisons, families etc. According to him, it was at these local sites that the practices of power were perfected; that it is because of this that power can have its global effects. And, he argued, it is at these local sites that the workings of power are most evident.

So, for Foucault, this modern system of power was decentred and "taken up", rather than centralized and exercised from the top down. Therefore, he argued that efforts to transform power relations in a society must address these practices of power at the local level – at the level of the every-day, taken-for-granted social practices.

Techniques of Power

In tracing the history of the apparatuses and institutions through which these practices were perfected, Foucault (1979) identifies Bentham's Panopticon as the "ideal" model for this form of power – for the:

> technologies of power, which determine the conduct of individuals and submit them to certain ends or domination, an objectivizing of the subject. (Foucault, 1988, p. 18)

I have discussed Foucault's analysis of this model elsewhere (White, 1989). This model establishes a system of power in which:

- *the source of power is invisible to those who experience it most intensely,*
- *persons are isolated in their experience of subjugation,*
- *persons are subject to the "gaze" and to "normalizing judgement",*
- *it is impossible for persons to determine when they are the subject of surveillance and scrutiny and when they are not, and therefore must assume this to always be the case,*
- *persons are incited to perpetually evaluate themselves, to police themselves and to operate on their bodies and souls to forge them as docile,*
- *power is autonomous to the extent that those participating in the subjugation of others are, in turn, the "instruments" of power.*

Foucault's analysis of the Panopticon provides an account of how the mechanisms and the structures of this modern system of power actually recruited persons into collaborating in the subjugation of their own lives and in the objectification of their own bodies; of how they became "willing" participants in the disciplining of, or policing of, their own lives. These mechanisms of this modern system of power recruit persons into what Foucault refers to as the

> technologies of the self, which permit individuals to effect by their own means or with the help of others a certain number of operations on their own bodies and souls, thoughts, conduct, and way of being so as to transform themselves in order to attain a certain state of happiness, purity, wisdom, perfection, or immortality. (1988, p. 18)

The ruse

However, this collaboration is rarely a conscious phenomenon. The workings of this power are disguised or masked because it operates in relation to certain norms that are assigned a "truth" status. This is a power that is exercised in relation to certain knowledges that construct particular truths, and is designed to bring about particular and "correct" outcomes, like a life considered to be "fulfilled", "liberated ", "rational", "differentiated", "individuated", "self-possessed", "self-contained", and so on.

The descriptions for these "desired" ways of being are in fact illusionary. According to Foucault, they are all part of a ruse that disguises what is actually taking place – these dominant truths are actually specifying of persons' lives and of relationships; those correct outcomes are particular ways of being that are prescribed ways of being.

So, the practices of modern power, as detailed by Foucault, are particularly insidious and effective. They incite persons to embrace their own subjugation; to relate to their own lives through techniques of power that are moulding of these lives, including their bodies and their gestures, according to certain "truths". The ways of being informed by these truths are not seen, by these persons, as the effect of power, but instead as the effect of something like fulfillment, of liberation.

Discussion

This analysis of power is difficult for many persons to entertain, for it suggests that many of the aspects of our individual modes of behaviour that we assume to be an expression of our free will, or that we assume to be transgressive, are not what they might at first appear. In fact, this analysis would suggest that many of our modes of behaviour reflect our collaboration in the control or the policing of our own lives, as well as the lives of others; our collusion in the specification of lives according to the dominant knowledges of our culture.

In undertaking his analysis of the "technologies of power" and the "technologies of the self", Foucault was not proposing that these were the only faces of power. In fact, in relation to fields of power, he proposed the study of four technologies: technologies of production, technologies of sign systems, technologies of power, and technologies of the self (Foucault, 1988).

Although I have followed Foucault in emphasizing the techniques of a modern "positive" system of power in this paper, I believe that other analyses of power, including those that relate to Bourdieu's thoughts about the structure of social systems of power and the constitutive effects of these structures on persons' stances in life, are highly relevant in the consideration of the everyday situations that are confronted by therapists.

Other considerations of fields of power would include the extent to which some of the structures that represent the earlier system of sovereign power still exist, and the extent to which institutional inequalities – those of a structural nature and those that relate to an inequality of opportunities – dominate our culture.

In fact, in his analysis of Bentham's Panopticon, Foucault draws attention to a structure that is at the heart of its operations. Upon considering the implications of this structure in terms of inequality, I have elsewhere suggested that, in our culture, men are more often likely to be the "instruments" of the normalizing gaze, and women more often likely to be the subject of this gaze (White, 1989). This point has also been made by other authors (e.g. Hare-Mustin, 1990).

The deconstruction of practices of power

In therapy, the objectification of these familiar and taken-for-granted practices of power contributes very significantly to their deconstruction. This is achieved by engaging persons in externalizing conversations about these practices. As these practices of power are unmasked, it becomes possible for persons to take a position on them, and to counter the influence of these practices in their lives and relationships.

These externalizing conversations are initiated by encouraging persons to provide an account of the effects of these practices in their lives. In these conversations, special emphasis is given to what these practices have dictated to persons about theft relationship with their own self, and about their relationships with others.

It is through these externalizing conversations that persons are able to:

(a) appreciate the degree to which these practices are constituting of their own lives as well as the lives of others,

(b) identify those practices of self and of relationship that might be judged as impoverishing of their lives, as well as the lives of others,

(c) acknowledge the extent to which they have been recruited into the policing of their own lives and, as well, the nature of their participation in the policing of the lives of others, and to

(d) explore the nature of local, relational politics.

It is through these externalizing conversations that persons no longer experience these practices as representative of authentic ways of being with themselves and with others. They no longer experience being at one with these practices, and begin to sense a certain alienation in relation to them. Persons are then in a position to develop alternative and preferred practices of self and of relationship – counter-practices. In therapy, I have participated with persons in challenging various practices of power, including those that relate to:

(a) the technologies of the self – the subjugation of self through the discipline of bodies, souls, thoughts, and conduct according to specified ways of being (including the various operations that are shaping of bodies according to the gender specific knowledges),

(b) the technologies of power – the subjugation of others through techniques such as isolation and surveillance, and through perpetual evaluation and comparison.

And I have also participated with persons in the deconstruction of particular modes of life and thought by reviewing, with them, the constitutive effects of the specific situation of their lives in those fields of power that take the form of social structures. In response to this, persons are able to challenge these effects, as well as those structures that are considered to be inequitable.

Examples

Perhaps it would be timely to return briefly to the stories about Amy and Robert. Amy had been recruited into certain practices of the government of the self – "technologies of the self". She had embraced these practices as a form of self-control, and as essential to the transformation of her life into an acceptable shape – one which spoke to her of fulfillment. She had construed her participation in activities in the subjugation of her own life as liberating activities.

Upon engaging Amy in an externalizing conversation about anorexia nervosa through the exploration of its real effects in her life, she began to identify the various practices of self-government – of the disciplines of the body – and the specifications for self that were embodied in anorexia nervosa. Anorexia was no longer her saviour. The ruse was exposed, and the practices of power were unmasked. Instead of continuing to embrace these practices of the self, Amy experienced alienation in relation to them. Anorexia nervosa no longer spoke to her of her identity. This opened up space for Amy to enter into activities that further subverted the realities constructed by anorexia nervosa, and into an exploration of alternative and preferred practices of self and of relationship.

To Robert, the unexamined and unquestioned knowledges, practices or "technologies of power", structures and conditions that provided the context for his abusive behaviour were all part of a taken-for-granted mode of life and thought that he had considered to be reflective of the natural order of things. Upon entering an externalizing conversation about these knowledges, practices, structures and conditions, and in mapping the real effects of these upon his own life and upon the lives of others, he experienced a separation from this mode of life and thought – this no longer spoke to him of the "nature" of men's ways of being with women and children.

Then, via a unique outcome as a point of entry, Robert was able to engage in an "archeology" of, and the performance of, alternative and preferred practices of relationship. As well, he began to challenge the structures and conditions that are supportive of men's abusive behaviour.

Knowledge practices

The professional disciplines have been successful in the development of language practices and techniques that determine that it is those disciplines that have access to the "truth" of the world. These techniques encourage persons in the belief that the members of these disciplines have access to an objective and unbiased account of reality, and of human nature[19]:

> What this means is that certain speakers, those with training in certain special techniques – supposedly to do with the powers of the mind to make contact with reality – are privileged

to speak with authority beyond the range of their personal experience. (Parker & Shotter, 1990, p. 7)

These language practices introduce ways of speaking and of writing that are considered to be rational, neutral and respectable, emphasizing notions of the authoritative account and the impersonal expert view. These practices disembody the perspective and the opinions of the speaker and the writer. The presentation of the knowledges of the speaker and writer is devoid of information that might give the respondent or the reader information about the conditions of the production of the expert view.

These practices of speaking and writing establish accounts of knowledges that are considered to be "global and unitary" (Foucault, 1980), accounts that mask the historical struggles associated with their ascendancy, including the multiplicity of resistances to them. It is difficult for persons to challenge these global and unitary knowledges because the language practices that constitute them include built-in injunctions against questions that might be raised about their socio/political/historical contexts.

Without this critical information, respondents/readers experience a certain "suspension". They do not have the information necessary to determine how they might "take" the views that are expressed, and this dramatically reduces the range of possible responses available to them. Respondents/readers can either subject themselves to the expert knowledge, or they can rail against it. Dialogue over different points of view is impossible.

For the members of the professional disciplines who are operating under the apprehension that they have recourse to objective knowledge, critical reflection on their position is not an option. Thus they are able to avoid facing the moral and ethical implications of their knowledge practices:

A description which contains no critical reflection on the position from which it is articulated can have no other principle than the interests associated with the unanalysed relation that the researcher has with this object. (Bourdieu, 1988, p. 15)

The open, vague, temporary and changing nature of the world is rendered, by these truth discourses, closed, certain, fixed and permanent. Other ways of speaking/writing are rendered invisible, or, as they are considered to be inferior, are mostly excluded. These "inferior" ways of speaking/writing are only acknowledged if accompanied by the "appropriate" deference to the warranted ways of speaking /writing.

The deconstruction of knowledge practices

Therapists can contribute to the deconstruction of expert knowledge by considering themselves to be "co-authors" of alternative and preferred knowledges and practices, and through a concerted effort to establish a context in which the persons who seek therapy are privileged as the primary authors of these knowledges and practices. Some of the "therapeutic" practices that are informed by this perspective follow. These by no means exhaust the possibilities, and David Epston and I have discussed other such therapeutic practices elsewhere (e.g. Epston & White, 1990; White & Epston, 1989).

Therapists can undermine the idea that they have privileged access to the truth by consistently encouraging persons to assist them in the quest for understanding. This can be achieved by giving persons notice of the extent to which the therapist's participation in therapy is dependent upon feedback from persons about their experience of the therapy. It is acknowledged that the person's experiences of therapy is essential to the guidance of the therapy, as this is the only way that a therapist can know what sort of therapeutic interaction is helpful and what is not.

This can be further emphasized if therapists engage persons in some inquiry as to why certain of the ideas that emerge during the interview interest those persons more than other ideas. What is it that persons find significant or helpful about the particular perspectives, realizations, conclusions etc? What preferred outcomes, for persons' lives, might accompany the particular perspectives, realizations, conclusions etc?

Therapists can challenge the idea that they have an expert view by continually encouraging persons to evaluate the real effects of the therapy in their lives and relationships, and to determine for themselves to what extent these effects are preferred effects and to what extent they are not. The feedback that arises from this evaluation assists therapists to squarely face the moral and ethical implications of their practices.

The therapist can call into question the idea that s/he possesses an objective and unbiased account of reality, and undermine the possibility that persons will be subject to the imposition of ideas, by encouraging persons to interview her/him about the interview. In response to this, the therapist is able to deconstruct and thus embody her/his responses (including questions, comments, thoughts, and opinions) by situating these in the context of his/her personal experiences, imagination, and intentional states. This can be described as a condition of "transparency"[20] in the therapeutic system, and it contributes to a context in which persons are more able to decide, for themselves, how they might take these therapist responses.

If the therapist is working with a reflecting team[21], at the end of the session this team can join with persons in interviewing the therapist about the interview. Apart from asking questions about the particular responses of the therapist, at this time team members can be invited to explore the therapist's thoughts about the actual process of the therapy across the interview.

The therapeutic practices of deconstruction and embodiment also hold for the responses of reflecting teams. Reflecting team members can be discouraged from engaging in the time-honoured structuralist and functionalist truth discourses of the psychotherapies, and encouraged to respond to those developments that are identified by family members as preferred developments, or to speculate about those developments that might be preferred.[22] Following this, reflecting team members can interview each other about their reflections so that they might situate these in the context of their personal experience, imagination and intentional states. The options and choices available to persons is maximized through this personalizing of the knowledges of the members of the reflecting team.

The deconstruction of the responses of the members of the reflecting team can be structured around questions like: What was it that caught your attention? Why do you think this caught your attention so? Why did this strike you as so significant? How did you decide to comment on this here? What effect did you think this comment would have?[23] What was your intention in asking this question here?

challenge experimate

This transparency of practice provides a challenge to the commonly accepted idea that for therapy to have its desired effects its workings need to be kept secret; the idea that if persons know what the therapist is up to then it won't work. On reviewing these practices with persons, I have learned that they often regard the embodiment of the therapist's and reflecting team's responses to be a highly significant factor in achieving the changes in their lives that they have valued most.

Conclusion

Those therapeutic practices that I refer to as "deconstructive" assist in establishing, for persons, a sense of "agency". This sense is derived from the experience of escaping "passengerhood" in life, and from the sense of being able to play an active role in the shaping of one's own life – of possessing the capacity to influence developments in one's life according to one's purposes and to the extent of bringing about preferred outcomes. This sense of personal agency is established through the development of some awareness of the degree to which certain modes of life and thought shape our existence, and through the experience of some choice in relation to the modes of life and thought that we might live by.

Those therapeutic practices that I refer to as deconstructive assist persons to separate from those modes of life and thought that they judge to be impoverishing their own lives and of the lives of others. And they provoke in therapists, and in the persons who seek therapy, a curiosity in regard to those alternative versions of who these persons might be. This is not just any curiosity. It is a curiosity about how things might be otherwise, a curiosity about that which falls outside of the totalizing stories that persons have about their lives, and outside of those dominant practices of self and of relationship.

An emphasis on curiosity in therapeutic practices is by no means new, and I would refer you to Gianfranco Cecchin's (1987) recasting of neutrality. I will leave you with one of Michel Foucault's delightful contributions on this subject:

Curiosity is a vice that has been stigmatized in turn by Christianity, by philosophy, and even by a certain conception of science. Curiosity, futility. The word, however, pleases me. To me it suggests something altogether different: it evokes "concern"; it evokes the care one takes for what exists and could exist; a readiness to find strange and singular what surrounds us; a certain relentlessness to break up our familiarities and to regard otherwise the same things; a fervor to grasp what is happening and what passes; a casualness in regard to the traditional hierarchies of the important and the essential. (1989, p. 198)

Notes

1. I prefer the description "sole parent" over the description "single parent". In our culture, It appears that "single" has so many negative connotations, including of incompleteness, of being unmarried, of failure – of not having made the grade. However, at least to my mind, the word "sole" conjures up something entirely different. It carries a recognition of the extraordinary responsibility that these parents face and of the strength necessary to achieve what they achieve. And, as well, a second meaning is not hard to discern – "soul". Soul is about essence, and for persons to refer to themselves as "soul parents" is for them to recognise the "heartfulness" that they provide, that their children depend upon to "see them through".

2. The work undertaken here did include exploration of the possibility that the children may have been abused by their father. The findings disconfirmed this as a possibility.

3. In part, this work is premised on the narrative metaphor which brings with it a specific non-essentialist account of authenticity. According to this metaphor, ordinarily a person achieves a sense of authenticity when (a) they perform particular claims about their lives, claims that relate to particular self-narratives, and when (b) this performance is witnessed by themselves or/and others. This would suggest that there is a range of possible authenticities that persons might experience, and that this range is determined by the available stock of stories that persons have about their lives.

4. David Epston, of Auckland, New Zealand, has joined with a number of persons who have sought therapy for anorexia nervosa, in establishing the "The Anti-Anorexia League". The aims of this league are to unmask the "voice" of anorexia

nervosa, and to identify, document, and circulate knowledges and practices that are counter to those knowledges and practices upon which the anorexia nervosa depends.

5. Initial steps in fieldwork should not be overly ambitious. Questions like this contribute to more humble beginnings and to increased possibilities in terms of the circulation and the authentication of alternative knowledges of self.

6. I would refer readers to Alan Jenkin's book, *Invitations to responsibility* (1990) for an excellent discussion of this and other aspects of work with men who abuse others.

7. The counselling of family members in relation to the abuse and other issues was undertaken concurrently in a different context.

8. I do not believe it is ever sufficient for men to take entire responsibility for perpetrating abuse, to identify the experience of those abused, to get in touch with the short-term and possible long-term effects of the abuse, to develop a sincere apology, to work on ways of repairing what might be repaired, and to challenge the attitudes that justify such behaviour and the conditions and techniques of power that make abuse possible.

    If that is where it ends, although the man may experience genuine remorse, he is likely to re offend because he has no other knowledges of men's ways of being to live by. For there to be any semblance of security that this will not occur, I believe that it is essential that these men be engaged in the identification and the performance of alternative knowledges of men's ways of being.

9. These representatives must be nominated by the child and the non-offending spouse, and they can be relatives who do not have a history of abusive behaviour, or persons known to them in the community.

10. Escape from secrecy meetings are held weekly in the first place, and gradually move to a monthly basis over a period of two years. At each of these meetings, events of the past week or so are reviewed. Events which reflect a reappearance of any of those attitudes, strategies, conditions, and structures that provided the context for past abuse can be identified and challenged.

    Different family members take turns at minute-taking for these meetings and in the posting of these minutes to the therapist (frequently with the assistance of the representatives). The family member whose turn it is to take this responsibility is encouraged to append their confidential comments to these minutes. If the therapist does not receive the minutes of a meeting on schedule, s/he immediately follows this up. From time to time the therapist joins these meetings to review progress.

    It is not possible to over-emphasise the importance of local accountability in this work. State intervention can be highly effective in bringing about the immediate cessation of abuse, but local accountability structures are essential to the establishment of secure contexts.

11. For an excellent discussion of the significance of secrecy. In structuring a context for abuse, I would refer readers to Lesley Laing and Amanda Kamsler's "Putting an end to secrecy" (1990).

12. Elsewhere I have referred to landscape of action questions as "unique account" questions, and to landscape of consciousness questions as "unique redescription" questions (White, 1988a).

13. Of course, the order of these questions can be reversed. Developments in the landscape of consciousness can be reviewed for what they might reveal about preferred developments in the landscape action. For example, "What did you see yourself doing that led you to this conclusion about your nature?" "What else have you witnessed yourself doing that reflects this belief?"

14. The re-vision of intentional states is often begun ahead of the introduction of these landscape of consciousness questions with the institution of externalizing conversations in relation to the problem. This is achieved through questions like: "What does this problem have you doing that is against your better judgement/ what you intend for your life/what you value/what you believe to be important?"

15. Daphne Hewson of the Macquarie University, Sydney, working from the perspectives of both narrative theory and social-cognitive psychology, has pioneered the development of prediction questions as a means of bringing forth the history of alternative stories (see Hewson, 1991).

16. What's in a word? Answer – a world! And I believe that, for therapists, the dramatic terms "act", "scene", "agents", "agency", and "purpose", introduce a different world to that world introduced by the terms "what, where, who, how, and why". The terms act and scene impart a sense of the constructed and thematic nature of the world, the terms agent and agency invoke ideas about specific "contributions" and a "know-how" that is related to intentional states, and the term purpose is suggestive of particular intentional states as explanatory notions.

17. Debra Milinsky of Berkeley, who has a strong interest in the history of such matters, informs me that the Etruscans can be most fairly credited for the development of the modern above-ground arch.

18. To my knowledge, there are a number of family therapists now undertaking a study of Derrida's work, and exploring the implications of his ideas in terms of therapeutic practices. Ron Findlay of St Kilda, Victoria, recently presented some of his thoughts on Derrida and therapy at a meeting at Dulwich Centre.

19. Feminist thinkers recognise these language practices as distinctly patriarchal, and seek to challenge them with an ethic of care, within an emphasis on context. For example, see Carol Gilligan's *In a different voice* (1982).

20. When discussing with David Epston how I might best depict this deconstruction of the therapist responses, he suggested the term "transparency".

21. For an introduction to the concept of the reflecting team, see Andersen (1987).

[22.] As with therapist re-authoring practices, reflecting team members orient themselves to unique outcomes as one might orient themself to mysteries. Thus, when team members make comments on unique outcomes, this is followed by questions and perceptions from within the team that are intended to engage the lived experience and imagination of family members in the unravelling of these mysteries. In this way, family members are privileged as the primary authors of alternative and preferred stories.

[23.] This question was suggested by Stephen Madigan during his visit to Dulwich Centre through the "Down Under Family Therapy Scholarship".

References

Andersen, T. (1987). The reflecting team: Dialogue and meta-dialogue in clinical work. *Family Process*, *26*(4), 415–428.

Bourdieu, P. (1988). *Homo Academicus*. Redwood City, CA: Stanford University Press.

Bruner, J. (1986). *Actual minds, possible worlds*. Cambridge, MA: Harvard University Press.

Bruner, J. (1990). *Acts of meaning*. Cambridge, MA: Harvard University Press.

Burke, K. (1969). *A grammar of motives*. Berkeley, CA: University of California Press.

Cecchin, G. (1987). Hypothesizing, circularity and neutrality revisited: An invitation to curiosity. *Family Process*, *26*(4), 405–413.

Derrida, J. (1981). *Positions*. Chicago, IL: University of Chicago Press.

Epston, D., & White, M. (1990). Consulting your consultants: The documentation of alternative knowledges. *Dulwich Centre Newsletter*, (4), 25–35.

Foucault, M. (1979). *Discipline and punish: The birth of the prison.* Middlesex, UK: Peregrine Books.

Foucault, M. (1980). *Power/knowledge: Selected interviews and other writings*. New York, NY: Pantheon Books.

Foucault, M. (1984). *The history of sexuality*. Middlesex, UK: Peregrine Books.

Foucault, M. (1988). Technologies of the self. In L. Martin, H. Gutman, & P. Hutton (Eds.), *Technologies of the self* (pp. 16-49). Amherst, MA: University of Massachusetts Press.

Foucault, M. (1989). *Foucault live*. New York, NY: Semiotext(e).

Geertz, C. (1986). Making experiences, authoring selves. In V. W. Turner & E. Bruner (Eds.), *The anthropology of experience* (pp. 373-380). Chicago, IL: University of Illinois Press.

Gilligan, C. (1982). *In a different voice.* Cambridge, MA: Harvard University Press.

Hare-Mustin, R. (1990). Sex, lies and headaches: The problem is power. In T. Goodrich (Ed.), *Women and power: Perspectives for therapy* (pp. 63-85). New York, NY: W. W. Norton.

Hewson, D. (1991). From laboratory to therapy room: Prediction questions for reconstructing the 'new-old' story. *Dulwich Centre Newsletter*, (3), 5–12.

Jenkins, A. (1990). *Invitations to responsibility: The therapeutic engagement of men who are violent and abusive.* Adelaide, Australia: Dulwich Centre Publications.

Laing, L & Kamsler, A. (1990). Putting an end to secrecy: Therapy with mothers and children following disclosure of child sexual assault. In M. Durrant & C. White (Eds.), *Ideas for therapy with sexual abuse* (pp. 157-179). Adelaide, Australia: Dulwich Centre Publications.

Parker, I., & Shotter, J. (Eds.) (1990). *Deconstructing social psychology.* London, UK: Routledge.

Turner, V. (1980). Social drama and stories about them. *Critical Inquiry*, (Autumn).

van Gennep, A. (1960). *The rites of passage.* Chicago, IL: Chicago University Press.

White, M. (1984). Pseudo-encopresis: From avalanche to victory, from vicious to virtuous cycles. *Family Systems Medicine, 2*(2), 150–160.

White, M. (1986). Negative explanation, restraint, and double description: A template for family therapy. *Family Process, 25*(2), 169–184.

White, M. (1988a). The process of questioning: A therapy of literary merit? *Dulwich Centre Newsletter*, (Winter), 8–14.

White, M. (1988b). Saying hullo again: The incorporation of the lost relationship in the resolution of grief. *Dulwich Centre Newsletter*, (Spring), 7–11.

White, M. (1989). The externalizing of the problem and the re-authoring of lives and relationships. *Dulwich Centre Newsletter*, (Summer), 3–21.

White, M., & Epston, D. (1989). *Literate means to therapeutic ends.* Adelaide, Australia: Dulwich Centre Publications. (Republished in 1990 as *Narrative means to therapeutic ends.* New York, NY: W. W. Norton.)

chapter two

Psychotic experience and discourse

An interview with Michael White by Ken Stewart

Ken: In the interview of 1990 I asked about your theory of pathology. You responded to this question with:

> *The word makes me wince! When I hear it, I think about the spectacular success of clinical medicine in the objectification of persons and of their bodies, and the extent to which the pathologising of persons is the most common and taken-for-granted practice in the mental health/welfare disciplines, and the central and most major achievement of the psychologies.*

Would your response be similar today?

Michael: I wouldn't take back what I said in that interview of a few years ago. There now exists a simply fantastic number of opportunities that are available to mental health professionals for the pathologising of people's lives. Due to an extraordinary investment in the development of the discourses of pathology, we now have at our disposal a vast array of ways of speaking with and interacting with people that reproduce the subject/object dualism that is so pervasive in the structuring of relations in our culture.

These ways of speaking and interacting with people puts them on the other side of knowledge, on the outside. These ways of speaking and acting make it possible for mental health professionals to construct people as the objects of psychiatric knowledge, to contribute to a sense of identity which has "otherness" as its central feature. The success of these discourses is beyond question, and I believe that this achievement represents one of the truly great marginalisations of contemporary culture.

Ken: In our field, we are currently seeing a great deal of interest in postmodern thought. Do you think these postmodern influences are having much of an impact on various pathologising discourses?

Michael: As you say, there have been significant developments of this sort. However, I'm not at all sure that these have yet gone very far in challenging the hegemony of the pathologising discourses, which are undergoing constant processes of revision, refinement and elaboration.

Ken: Where does this leave us? Is there a way to address traditional conceptions of the so-called mental illnesses such as schizophrenia, obsessive-compulsive disorder, the histrionic personality disorder, and other personality disorders from the Axis II personality disorders of the DSM-IV, without pathologising people? Do those of us who embrace the social constructionist perspective have to leave this domain to the authors of the psychiatric knowledges, or do we make some kind of counter-claim to this territory? And, if we do, how do we address the phenomena that these classifications refer to? Do you think that family therapy has something to offer here?

Michael: Perhaps I could take your last question first. For some reason, in the critique of the institutions that have played a key role in the maintenance and in the reproduction of these pathologising discourses, family therapy exempts itself. It has so often considered itself on the outside of these discourses of pathology. But I do not believe that family therapy's claim to this exempt status can be sustained.

Historically, family therapy has embraced formal systems of analysis that are informed by the metaphors of "system", "dynamics", "structure", and so on. These metaphors provide for an "expert" interpretation of the events and of the experiences of people's lives, and have been deployed to invoke notions of family or relational "disorder", "dysfunction", and "pathology". And these metaphors have encouraged us to position ourselves in relation to others in a way that also reproduces the subject/object dualism that I have already referred to.

Ken: There have been many critiques of these, and other pathologising discourses – both from within and outside the field. Yet, despite this, they continue to dominate all other discourses that have tried to offer alternatives. How do you understand this?

Michael: Yes, there have been many critiques. Perhaps it would be useful here to review one or two of these.

First, there is the issue of the self-presentation of the mental health professional. It has been said that to demonstrate a degree of "mastery" in the ways of speaking about other people's lives that are informed by these pathologising discourses, and to demonstrate a degree of skill in those ways of acting towards others that are informed by these discourses, accords these professionals a small grant of moral worth in their own communities. The achievement of this mastery, and the demonstration of this skill, brings with it the experience of esteem in the eyes of one's colleagues.

Second, it has been argued that to demonstrate this mastery and these skills opens the door to a world of career opportunities, and to economic opportunities. So, the demonstration of "diagnostic acumen" turns out to be highly rewarding – it is lucrative and it provides access to institutional power. But, more than this, here in North America it has become a necessity. It is now becoming virtually impossible for mental health professionals to earn a living if they don't subject their work to the DSM III-R, or whatever the latest version of this is.

Third, it can be argued that, since the pathologising discourses are cloaked in an impressive language that establishes claims to an objective reality, these discourses make it possible for mental health professionals to avoid facing the real effects of, or the consequences of, these ways of speaking about and acting towards those people who consult them. If our work has to do with the idea of subjecting persons to "truth", then this renders invisible to us the consequences of how we speak to people about their lives, and of how we structure our interactions with them; this mantle of "truth" makes it possible for us to avoid reflecting on the implications of our constructions and of our therapeutic interactions in regard to the shaping of people's lives. In this way, pathologising discourses make it possible for mental health professionals to avoid accountability, and to retain and to extend on their monopoly on power.

These are but a few of the many possible critiques. But, aside from these, there are other considerations that may account for the extraordinary development of, and success of, these pathologising discourses. Pathologising discourses have the potential to bring to us a degree of comfort in a world in which it is becoming increasingly difficult to find this. These discourses make it possible to define those problems for which people seek help as aberrations. As such, they assist us to avoid the acknowledgement of the fact that these problems are very significantly of our culture, that these problems are products of our modes of life and of thought. The discourses of pathology make it possible for us to ignore the extent to which the problems for which people seek therapy are the outcome of certain practices of relationship and practices of the self, many of which are actually informed by modern notions of "individualism". And the discourses of pathology make it possible for us to ignore the extent to which the problems for which people seek help are so often mired in the structures of inequality of our culture, including those pertaining to gender, race, ethnicity, class, economics, age, and so on.

If we can see the difficulties for which people seek help as the outcome of some aberration rather than a product of our ways of thought and ways of life, we can avoid facing our complicity in the maintenance of these ways of life and of thought. This assists us to disavow our complicity in the constitution of the worlds we share with others. In obscuring this link between the problems for which people seek help and the modes of life and thought of our culture, we can avoid facing the responsibility that we have to take action to address the context of people's lives, and we can avoid facing the responsibility that we have to dismantle the various structures of inequality that are associated with these.

Ken: Okay. So, let's get down to some of the specifics of your work. I've heard it said that you are opposed to the use of labels and to the use of medications.

Michael: Now that's interesting. I've heard the very same opinion about my position on these matters.

Ken: Well?

Michael: From time to time I hear things about what I have said that I haven't spoken of, and from time to time I read accounts of my thought that do not relate to what I think. And at times I hear accounts of my conduct that are not at all close to my experience of it.

Ken: What's an example of this last point?

Michael: Several years ago, there was a story going around that, during a consultation in Canada, I had externalized a problem with a person who had a diagnosis of paranoid schizophrenia, and that, in response to this, I had been beaten up. What actually did happen was that I had intervened in an assault, in order to prevent the perpetration of grievous bodily harm, and had my face split open in the process. Furthermore, none of this had anything to do with a consultation.

Ken: Sounds simply awful! So tell me, what is your position on labels and medication?

Michael: In regard to drugs, I have not taken a general position on the so-called anti psychotic medications. Instead, I have been far more interested to find what is enabling for people in regard to this question – and here I am using the word "enabling" in its positive sense. This consideration leads to specific questions:

- *How might one go about assisting people to determine whether these drugs are contributing to their quality of life, or whether they are subtracting from this?*
- *How might one go about assisting people to determine in which ways these drugs might be enabling, and in which ways they might be disabling?*
- *How might one go about assisting people to monitor the effects of different medications, and of different levels of these medications?*
- *How might one go about assisting people to evaluate the real effects of these medications on their lives and in their relationships with others?*

- *How might one go about assisting people to establish what might be for them suitable criteria for such an evaluation?*

- *How might one go about assisting people to fully inform themselves about the various negative side-effects of these drugs?*

- *How might one go about assisting people to identify which people are most invested in compliance with regimes of medications, which people are least invested in this, and the particular interests of these parties?*

These are just a sample of the many, many questions that can be appropriately asked about drugs.

I do hope that this discussion goes some way towards challenging the view that I am opposed to the use of drugs. I have witnessed drugs being used in ways that have a profound effect in opening up the horizons of people's lives, in ways that bring a range of new possibilities for action. And I have also witnessed drugs being used in ways that are primarily far the purposes of social control, in ways that subtract very significantly from people's possibilities for action, in ways that dispossess people of choice.

Ken: And what are your thoughts on various labels used in the field of mental health?

Michael: If you are talking about making psychiatric diagnoses, I have no interest whatsoever in trafficking in this trade. In regard to labels in general, and people's use of them, questions similar to those we have just been talking about with regard to drugs seem appropriate.

In responding to questions of this sort, I am mindful of the fact that some people do find such labels enabling. This has been interpreted in a variety of ways. For example, it is said that illness labels undermine the various self-accusations and attributions of personal inadequacy that are experienced by people who are not able to live out their lives in the customary ways. Furthermore, it is said that these labels make it possible for persons to break from the stress of the expectations that they would be subject to if they were "well". And it is frequently argued that psychiatric diagnoses serve to dissolve the guilt that is so often experienced by relatives, and that this has the effect of undermining self-defeating behaviours and of promoting more constructive interactions in familial contexts.

And, while I can appreciate these arguments, and have no difficulty in honouring what people have to say about some of the positive effects of psychiatric diagnoses, I have no doubt that these outcomes provide for some interesting reflection on our culture – that, in order for people to break from these self-accusations and attributions of personal inadequacy, from the stress that is informed by the expectations about what it means to be a real person in our culture, and from the experiences of guilt that we have discussed, they must step into the site of "illness". Illness is a site of culture, one that is structured, one that brings with it particular modes of life and of thought. It is a site of culture that shapes life.

So, diagnosis provides for an exemption that is permissible through illness. But this is a sad reflection on our culture, and I do think that we can do a lot to assist people to find other alternative sites in this culture in which they can succeed in breaking from dominant ways of being and thinking, alternative sites that bring with them other options for how they might lead their lives, options that do not require exemption through illness.

And it is very interesting that, in the work that we do together to identify these other sites, sites that are often defined through the tracing of histories of resistance to dominant culture, the diagnosis itself becomes increasingly irrelevant, and the exemption it brings with it becomes increasingly unnecessary for living.

Ken: So, what happens when you are consulted by people who seem to identify with their psychiatric diagnosis?

Michael: I do not want to be misunderstood on this point. If I am consulting with a person who prefers to use such labels, then I am interested in honouring what they experience this to be doing for them, and I am interested in actively exploring with them what speaking about themselves in this way makes possible.

Ken: But, since these labels co-operate in the colonising of people's lives – treating them as an "other" that is at once "knowable and visible" – I would have assumed that you would be opposed to them altogether.

Michael: Well, it is difficult to be in opposition· to labels *per se*. In language, there is always naming, and so we always have labels of one sort or another. What is of critical importance, however, is the nature of the discourses that are associated with this naming. A consideration of discourse takes us to specific questions about any naming. What knowledges are privileged in a particular process of naming, and what knowledges are rendered irrelevant or are disqualified in this process? Who is qualified to speak and to name, and under what circumstances is it acceptable for them to do so? What relational practices and techniques of power are associated with acts of naming, of diagnosing, and what are the real effects, on people's lives, of these practices and techniques? And so on. Here I have been trying to emphasise the extent to which it is discourse that is of vital consideration.

Of course, the labels associated with one discourse can be usurped by taking them up into alternative discourses. This is often achieved by marginalised groups. When these labels are taken up and inserted into an alternative discourse, they often become terms of pride, and ones that represent certain lifestyle choices and knowledges about ways of being and thinking. This has the effect of taking such labels a long way from the mainstream discourse that had been so subjugating of people in marginalised groups.

Ken: So then, in my mind at least, these thoughts take me to considerations of aetiology. What is your position on aetiology?

Michael: In seventeen of the last twenty or so years I have had formal relations with mainstream psychiatric services – I have worked in state psychiatric hospitals and in child and adolescent psychiatric services, and have spent a considerable period of time consulting to a large state psychiatric hospital. And, in addition to this, at Dulwich Centre we have a small independent community mental health project. Now, let me tell you something that you might find surprising. Throughout this entire period, in the totality of my experience of these different psychiatric contexts, the only times that I have witnessed considerations of aetiology having any effect on management whatsoever have been on those relatively few occasions upon which a brain lesion of some sort has been suspected. Even medication is a trial-and-error affair. I say that you might find this surprising, because, despite the general irrelevance of considerations of aetiology, anyone who has worked for mainstream psychiatric services will have witnessed an extraordinary amount of time and energy devoted to these considerations.

So, what are we to conclude about this? Perhaps such considerations of aetiology are a hallmark of the performance of psychiatric knowledge because these considerations provide opportunities for the scientising of this knowledge.

Ken: So, you don't have a position on aetiology?

Michael: To answer your question, I have always resisted taking a position on the aetiology of the so-called psychiatric disorders. In fact, I have consistently refused the incitement that I have experienced to step into a position on this, and to enter into debates and other activities that depend upon such positions. I am willing to consider most notions of aetiology, but, quite frankly, these considerations are as irrelevant to what I do in this work as they are for others.

Ken: Does this mean that you are even willing to entertain some of the current biological notions of aetiology for what is referred to as schizophrenia?

Michael: Of course! Of course! But this is not relevant to what I do.

Ken: So, what do you do? In taking the position that you do on psychiatric discourses, isn't there a risk that you wind up excluding yourself from participation in this field? Isn't it possible that, in this way, you will cancel out your own contribution? Doesn't this leave you with nothing to say?

Michael: Certainly not. I am simply talking about standing outside of the territory as it is defined by psychiatric knowledge, and as it is structured by pathologising discourses. I am not talking about standing apart from people and their experiences, including those experiences that are so often taken up into pathologising discourses.

Ken: Okay, what are our options?

Michael: I think that we can assist people to challenge the hegemony of the psychiatric knowledges. We can work with them to identify the extent that their own lives are "knowledged". We can engage people in conversations that are honouring of their knowledges of life, and that trace the history of their knowledgeableness. We can join people in conversations that provide the opportunity for them to build on these knowledges, and that assist people to develop plans for applying this knowledgeableness to those experiences that they find troubling.

We can make it our business to work collaboratively with people in identifying those ways of speaking about their lives that contribute to a sense of personal agency, and that contribute to the experience of being an authority on one's life. And we can assist people to draw distinctions around these ways of speaking and those other ways of speaking that contribute to experiences of marginalisation, that subtract from a sense of personal agency, and that undermine an appreciation of one's authoritativeness.

Rather than referencing what we do to the sort of formal systems of analysis that we have already discussed, we can strive to build on those developments in our work that are more referenced to people's experiences of life, including of psychotic phenomena. We can find ways of attending more directly to people's experiences of life.

And we can join with people in challenging those relations of power that inform the subject/object dualism that I referred to earlier in this conversation.

Ken: Take this last point. Say something more about how this might be achieved.

Michael: I'll float one example here, one that relates to the idea of returning the "gaze", or turning the gaze back on itself. For those people who are the recipients of ward rounds, for them to research these ward rounds can be very empowering. This might engage them in a study of who can speak, under what circumstances they can speak, which ways of speaking are acknowledged, which ways of speaking are disqualified, whose authority is privileged, the effects of the privileging of this voice, and so on. I find that many people are quite taken by the introduction of this idea, and that it has a positive effect even if it is not taken up in any formalised way. It appears that even to think the unthinkable goes some way towards undoing the effects of the marginalisation to which people have been subject. Of course, there are many other ways in which the gaze can be returned.

Ken: This is a subversive idea if I ever heard one.

Michael: Yes, this might be quite subversive. But practices of returning the gaze do not have to be covert, and they are not necessarily antagonistic to the efforts of the staff of psychiatric institutions. In fact, these practices can serve mental health professionals well in their efforts to establish contexts that are healing. In that these practices of returning the gaze can have the effect of rendering transparent many of the otherwise taken-for-granted ideas and practices of psychiatric contexts, they can be of great assistance to staff who experience a commitment to confront the moral and ethical responsibility for the real effects of their interactions on the lives of those people who are seeking help. When mental health professionals accept the fact that they can never be certain that they are not reproducing, in their work, the circumstances that provide the context of the very problems for which people are seeking help, they will experience a degree of relief in the feedback and the possibilities for action that are afforded by these practices of returning the gaze.

Ken: You also mentioned possibilities for being more experience-based in working with people who have defined psychiatric conditions. So, could you give me an example of what this experience-based work might look like with schizophrenia? And could you also say what distinguishes this from accepted approaches to this phenomenon?

Michael: In regard to the generally accepted approaches, I have noted a strong bias in regard to the psychotic experience itself. This is an anti-experience bias. I believe that the idea of talking to people about their psychotic experiences has had rather bad press over the past few decades. Within this context, it is not surprising that some of the proposals that I have put forward on talking to people about their subjective experience of psychotic episodes have provoked disquiet.

Ken: Maybe some fear that you would be reifying the delusions instead of talking people out of them. How has this sort of response impacted on your work?

Michael: It hasn't really. Some have expressed their apprehension about my practices of relating to psychotic experience, and, at times, have been somewhat perturbed by my unwillingness to desist in my further exploration of ways of talking to people about their experience of psychotic episodes. However, I have never found the content of such responses to be at all persuasive.

Ken: In some of your workshops, you have referred to the work that you do in assisting people to revise their relationship with their auditory hallucinations, or their "voices". Is this one of the developments that has come from this exploration of psychotic experiences?

Michael: Yes it is. Assisting people to revise their relationship with their voices is usually a very significant part of the interactions that I have with people who have the diagnosis of schizophrenia. The successful revision of this relationship invariably has a powerful effect on the quality of these people's lives, and, in my experience, it generally plays a considerable role in reducing their vulnerability to relapse as well.

Ken: If this is so, is this a practice that is being taken up more by mental health professionals?

Michael: Yes. I have contact with many mental health professionals who have been taking these ideas up in unique contexts and in unique ways.

As an example of how this is being done in working with groups of people who have psychiatric diagnoses and who are considered to be "chronically ill", I would refer you to the Worthy of Discussion groups of Gaye Stockell and Marilyn O'Neil from Sydney, and to the developments that they and their colleagues have been putting together in establishing more collaborative approaches in the rehabilitation context.

And I have contact with others who are enthusiastically exploring the fit between some of these ideas and practices, their own original contributions, and some of the more established ideas and practices in this field. For an example of such work I would refer you to Chris Beels and Margaret Newmark of New York, and to David Moltz of Portland, Maine.

As well, I know some administrators, managers, and clinical directors who have been effective in changing the face of the broader provision of psychiatric services by incorporating the sort of ideas and practices referred to here with a number of other related ideas and practices. A good person for you to talk to, who has achieved a great deal in this area, is Alan Rosen of Sydney.

But there are many other initiatives apart from these. One quite recent initiative is the work that Stephen Madigan, David Epston and the Anti-Anorexia League have been doing together in British Columbia – work that is having what I understand to be a transformative effect on policy with regard to the treatment of anorexia nervosa and bulimia.

Ken: These developments all sound exciting, and I would like to learn more about them. So I take it you haven't been too discouraged in your work in this area?

Michael: Definitely not. Over the years, I have experienced a good measure of support and encouragement from many people, and this has been sustaining.

However, I will say that my efforts to share more generally, with others, what people have had to say about this work have yielded mixed responses. So, at times, I haven't found things all that straightforward.

Ken: Give me an example of what you mean.

Michael: Well, in regard to the work that I have been developing on the revision of people's relationship with their voices, for some years, in certain circles, I did experience constraints in presenting my findings. These constraints were partly born of scepticism and of doubt, and were partly political in nature.

However, several years ago, articles began to be published in mainstream journals that called attention to the need to consider the subjective experience of those persons who received a diagnosis of schizophrenia, and that also called attention to the significance of the quality of the person's relationship with their voices. In fact, one journal devoted an entire issue to these explorations (see the *Schizophrenia Bulletin*, Volume 15, Number 2, 1989). While these articles did not describe processes that contributed to possibilities for people to revise their relationship with their voices, some of the findings were supportive of what I was doing, and, since the publication of articles like these, I have found it somewhat easier to talk about this work in psychiatric contexts.

Ken: So how do you explain this – that having a different relationship with one's voices can make a significant difference in terms of the severity of the psychotic episode?

Michael: In part, I believe that it relates to culture. Although it seems relatively easy for us to entertain the idea that much of what we think and believe, and much of what we do, is informed by culture, for some reason it seems rather more difficult for us to entertain the idea that psychotic phenomena are similarly informed; that, regardless of aetiology, the content, form and expression of psychotic phenomena, such as auditory hallucinations, are shaped by culture. When it becomes less difficult to entertain this idea, it becomes possible for us to appreciate the extent to which culture is just as shaping of the lives of people who have whatever it is that schizophrenia is.

Ken: Give me an example of this.

Michael: There is nothing about physiology or genetics that would predispose the voices of schizophrenia to attack their female subjects on the basis of their sexuality, or to call their male subjects "wimps". And there is nothing about physiology that would predispose the voices of schizophrenia to see others as adversaries, and their subjects as possessions. Those auditory hallucinations that people find most troublesome are so often distinctly patriarchal in their attitudes and their techniques of power. This is so for the voices that harass men and those that harass women. These voices are overwhelmingly evaluative of people; they are critical and disqualifying; they rate highly on expectations of people and low on acknowledgement.

Ken: You state that these voices are distinctly patriarchal. Could you say more about how they speak?

Michael: Okay, but I would like to emphasise the fact that I am not referring to all of the voices of schizophrenia here. In this work, it is essential to assist people to distinguish those voices that are controlling and dominating from those voices that are supportive, or that at least have the potential to be supportive.

Ken: Alright, but I would like to come back to this distinction later.

Michael: Those voices that are troublesome are highly opinionated and quite convincing. They rely on certain devices in order to speak impressively, in order to secure unquestionable authority, in order to establish claims to objective knowledge, in order to convince their subject that they alone can grasp the truth of people's natures, desires, purposes, and so on.

Ken: Can you say more about these devices? They sound scary.

Michael: The impressive ways of speaking to which I am referring are "at large", and we could refer to them as the "disembodied" ways of speaking. I am sure that these will be familiar to the readers of the transcript of this interview. These ways of speaking have been called disembodied because they disclaim any reference to context, because they allow one to establish knowledge claims that are considered to be context-independent. They have the effect of elevating specific knowledge claims to a certainty or "truth" status, and of disqualifying those knowledges that are represented in more situated ways of speaking.

Ken: Ah, yes – those who claim to speak the "truth" about all situations, regardless of context, an all-too-familiar experience that many of us have been subjected to. Still, I think that recent developments in the field have attempted to expose these "temptations of certainty". Could you say more about this kind of a-contextual way of speaking.

Michael: The devices that are associated with these "expert" ways of speaking include those that (a) obscure the motives or purposes that are associated with one's speech acts, (b) delete all reference to the personal experiences through which one's knowledge claims are generated, (c) exclude information about the personal and interpersonal struggles and dilemmas that are associated with the construction of one's preferred realities (this includes the erasure of the personal experiences of contestation and argumentation through which one's knowledge claims are established), (d) divert attention from the personal investments that are informed by one's location in the social worlds of gender, race, culture, class, work, sexual preference, and so on, and (e) delete all reference to the history of controversy and dissent that surrounds all "global" knowledge claims.

Ken: And what are the implications of this in this work?

Michael: Well, disembodied speech acts can be very disempowering of those who are subject to them. They are quite capturing. They severely limit and constrict possible responses. However, the persuasiveness and impressiveness of such speech acts can be undermined by the principle of embodiment; that is, by situating these speech acts within the context of the speaker's (a) motives and purposes, (b) personal experiences, including those that relate to dilemmas and other struggles that the speaker has experienced in the process of attributing meaning to their experiences of life, (c) investments that are informed by their location in the social worlds of gender, culture, race, class, sexual preference, and so on, and also by bringing forth the history of controversy that surrounds the speaker's objective knowledge claims.

Ken: Knowing your work as I do, I'll bet that you have some interesting questions that would uncover and deconstruct some of these truth claims.

Michael: Yes. We can ask questions that insist on embodiment, questions that require speakers to situate their opinions.

Ken: Could you give some examples of these questions?

Michael: Okay. To encourage speakers to situate their opinions in the context of their purposes, we could ask questions like: *So you have a strong opinion about what I should do. Tell me, in voicing your opinion in this way, what effect do you hope this might have on what I do?* Or maybe we could ask: *If you were to succeed in influencing what I do on this occasion, how would this fit with your overall goals for my life?* Or perhaps: *I think that I have some understanding of how you would like your opinion to shape what I do right now. How does this fit with your general purposes for my life? How does this fit with your plans for my life?*

To encourage speakers to situate their opinions in the context of their lived experience, we could try something like: *Could you tell me about some of your personal experiences of life that have played a central role in the formation of this opinion? This would be helpful to me, as I would then know more about how to take your opinion, and I might be able to identify those parts of your views that could fit for me. Perhaps I could then talk of some of my own experiences of life, and share with you some of the conclusions that I have reached from all of this.*

To encourage speakers to situate their opinions within the context of their location in the social world, we might try something like: *In which circles are these sort of opinions most strongly held? Do all of the people in these circles agree with this opinion? If some of these people were here with us, how would they go about supporting your opinion? What do you think would happen if, in their presence, you were to dissent? What sort of pressure do you think you would experience to conform, to recant? What consequences do you think you would be facing if you didn't agree to do so?*

But this is just a small sample of the possibilities for ways of responding that are deconstructing of the "truths" that are championed in disembodied speech acts. And I want to emphasise that these questions do not require an answer in order to be effective. In asking such questions, those who are subject to disembodied speech acts become less captive, and are confronted with new possibilities for action.

Ken: Those are great questions! I have some ideas about how I can put some to use right away. Members of my team often come across persons in social service or medical circles for whom these questions would be very appropriate. Can you tie these ideas back to the question of working with people who experience auditory hallucinations?

Michael: As I have already mentioned, when these voices are most troublesome, they speak impressively and persuasively. At the times that these voices are most troublesome, they succeed in convincing their subjects that they speak with authority, with objective knowledge; that they speak of the truth of life and of the world, of the truth of their subject's identity, of the truth of the motives of others, and so on. These impressive voices so often succeed in capturing their subject, and in disqualifying their subject's special knowledges of life. And this is usually traumatising and disempowering of everyone concerned.

In these circumstances it makes sense to de-authorise these impressive voices, to disempower them, and this can be achieved through the embodiment of their "truths". We can encourage the people who are the subjects of these voices to insist that the voices embody their demands, requirements, opinions, investments, and so on. Such embodiment can be achieved by assisting those who are in the subject position to situate these voices within the context of the voices' purposes, their experiences, and their history.

Ken: You speak of these voices as if they are independent entities.

Michael: Yes. In fact, in this work, the deconstruction of the "truths" of these voices can be achieved best through the personification of them. Or perhaps I should say that this is achieved through the extension of this personification, as it is not at all unusual for those people who are the subjects of these voices to have personified them in advance of our meeting – except that the purposes of these voices have not, until this time, been at all transparent.

Ken: Many people understand your work primarily involving various aspects of externalizing conversations with people – in which the problem is not only externalized, but personified in unique ways. This fits with other theorists and clinicians who speak of internalized voices and "objects" or representations of significant persons and relationships in our lives. So you externalize the hidden, more pernicious, aspects of what previously had been internalized or introjected. Is this way of personifying the problem a regular part of your practice?

Michael: Let me answer your question this way. This practice of personification is but one way of re-voicing the problem, and, for me, this re-voicing of the problem is an important aspect of the work that I do. I know that if we engage with people in the re-voicing of the problems that they consult us about, this provides them, and us as well, with the opportunity to establish an appreciation of the politics of the person's experience of life.

Ken: So, how do you proceed, in practice, with this re-voicing of the problem?

Michael: Mostly via the formulation of questions like:

- *What is it that the voices are trying to convince you of at this time? What are they trying to talk you into? How does this fit with their overall plans for your life?*
- *How do the voices expect their assertions, their "shoulds", to affect what you do? If they succeed in forcing their will on your life, how do you imagine this might influence the direction of your life?*
- *Are these voices for you having your own opinion, knowing what you want, or are they against you having your own opinion?*

• *I do appreciate that these voices throw you into confusion. In whose service is this confusion? Does it contribute to their goals for your life, or does this favour or clarify your own goals?*

As you can see, through questions like this, distinctions can be drawn around different desires, purposes, intentions, goals, and so on. These distinctions make it more possible for people to determine the extent to which these fit with the designs of the dominant voices, and the extent to which they fit with the sort of designs that are preferred by the person concerned. Even confusion is found to be in the service of these voices, rather than in the service of the person. In drawing such distinctions, persons achieve some degree of clarity about a preferred account of what they want for their life, and they are no longer so much at sea.

Ken: I like these questions. Not only do they externalize the voices, but they raise the question of whether or not they support opinions that are favoured by the person, or some other opinion that is different, and often opposed to the one that is preferred. One of the things that I find attractive about your work and writing is the attention you pay to relational politics and the techniques of power. Do you see a place for putting these ideas to work here?

Michael: Definitely. Exposing and describing the tactics that the voices employ to achieve what they achieve can be very helpful. These tactics can include all of those that make possible the privileging of one knowledge above others. And, when the chips are down, when their authority is at risk, these tactics also include various forms of abuse, terrorisation, subterfuge, treachery, pettiness, and so on.

Ken: That's interesting. Just how far are you willing to go, or how far are you prepared to extend, this re-voicing of the problem?

Michael: To reiterate, these voices rely upon time-honoured and disembodied speech acts for their influence. They draw attention to the motives of others, while disguising their own. In going to some lengths in the personifying of the voices, we open the possibilities for the deconstruction of, and unmasking of, all of this. In rendering transparent the voices' purposes in this way, people are assisted to revise their relationship with their voices. This personification also makes it more possible for us to assist people to monitor the progress of this revision in their relationship with their voices:

- *At this very moment, how are the voices coping with this exposure? To speak of them in this way, to unmask them in broad daylight, how does this affect them? Do you think that this is playing a part in reducing their influence, or playing a part in increasing this?*
- *Are the voices protesting this discussion? Has this unsettled them? Is this threatening to them? How we they reacting to the threat? Are they trying to "up the ante"? What do you think it means that they are threatened by this conversation?*
- *What is it like for the voices to have to listen to your thoughts for a change? What is it like for them to know that you are developing a disrespect for them and a mistrust of them – that you are on to their tricks of persuasion? How does this affect your position in your own life? Does it strengthen it, or weaken it?*

And so on.

Ken: Have others found these practices to be rather unusual?

Michael: Yes. And, as well, I want to be transparent about the fact that these practices have, as I have already mentioned, aroused some concerns. It has been said that I am somehow playing a role in the verification of what amounts to hallucinations, and thus culpable in the reinforcement of them. It has been argued that the problem with auditory hallucinations is that they are already externalized and that people need to own them, to integrate them – that the voices of schizophrenia really represent parts of the person that the person needs to integrate, thoughts that the person needs to come to terms with as their own, and so on. But these criticisms are based on modern notions of a "self" that is the centre of and source of all meaning, on notions of a unitary and essential self. And I do not believe that there is any hope whatsoever of sustaining this modern notion of the self.

Ken: So, if I understand you correctly, you encourage people to confront the voices. Does this ever take a form of the two-chair work that is common to Gestalt approaches?

Michael: No, definitely not. I am proposing something that is on the other side of these approaches – on the other side of such approaches at the levels of ideas, purpose, and practice. As I have said, the work to which I am referring is definitely not informed by the modern notions of the self, or by fashionable cultural notions about states of "wholeness" that might be achieved through "integration".

And there is no confrontation. Situations of direct conflict with these voices are avoided. In the practices that I am outlining in this discussion, there are no stand-offs. Highly emotive and stressful interactions are never encouraged. This would be entirely counter-productive. Rather, this work encourages people to take up an observer or self-reflexive position in relation to their own lives, a position in which they become the narrator of events in their relationship with the voices. Initially, this assists people to "suss out" the voices, and engages them in piecing together an exposé.

Ken: So, rather than integrating the so-called "split-off" parts of a single "self", as we might see in Gestalt approaches or even psychoanalytic approaches, you seem to be working to exclude the voices from people's lives.

Michael: The goal of this work is not to get rid of the hostile voices, but to assist people to revise their relationship with them, so that the voices' degree of influence is lessened. When people are in the subject position in regard to hostile voices, we can predict a deteriorating or relapsing course. When people break from the subject position, or when the voices are entered into the subject position, then we can predict improvements in the quality of people's lives, and fewer relapses.

However, as this work proceeds, it is not at all unusual for people to begin to report that the hostile voices absent themselves from their lives for significant periods. Because this is not an explicit goal, this sort of outcome is responded to as one of the bonuses of this work.

Ken: Back to what you were saying about confrontation, aren't there any occasions upon which direct confrontation would be indicated or useful?

Michael: Very rarely, and even then this would not take the form of a fight or a contest. Of course, at times people experience a strong temptation to enter the fray when they are experiencing the voices tantrumming, particularly when this is precipitated by a threat to the voices' position when there is a chance that the voices might lose their "foothold" in their subject's life. But people are not encouraged to reciprocate. Instead, they stand back, consult their documents of identity or read transcripts of therapy sessions, and let these tantrums play themselves out. It is from this position, outside of the fray, that people become aware of various options for resistance.

Ken: You mentioned earlier that it can be helpful to assist persons to discriminate those voices that are supportive, or at least potentially supportive, from those voices that are hostile. Say more about this.

Michael: I believe that people who are subject to psychotic phenomena that are traumatising can do with all the support they can get, even if some of this support is to be found within the psychotic experience itself. It is not unusual for people in these circumstances to report that some of the voices they experience seem genuinely concerned for their wellbeing, even if they are at times somewhat misguided in their attempts to demonstrate this concern. Now, it is possible to assist people to more clearly distinguish these friendly or potentially friendly voices from the hostile voices, and to develop a stronger alliance with these more supportive voices, one in which they become better informed about what is in the person's best interest.

Such alliances can play a significant role in that they provide people with support and with the experience of a solidarity of purpose. This renders them less vulnerable to the insecurity that the hostile or dominating voices provoke and rely upon to achieve a position of influence in the person's life.

Ken: How do people go about developing a stronger alliance with the more supportive voices?

Michael: Well, after the identification of those voices that are friendly, or at least potentially friendly, people can be assisted to elaborate on the character of these to the point that they take on the identity of an invisible friend.

Ken: And when they can say something about the character of the friendly voice, the voice takes on greater depth and complexity, and is able to be more easily sustained and adopted. Would you say this is a key part of this work?

Michael: No. It is simply helpful, but by no means essential. And, of course, there are many people who do not experience such friendly or potentially friendly voices.

Ken: Are there any other ways that alliances could be developed which would help people who are vulnerable to hostile voices, say, for people who do not experience friendly or even potentially friendly voices?

Michael: Many. For example, we can explore the possibilities for the generation of relationships with invisible friends. It is possible to work with people around the invention of an invisible friend, and at times it is even possible to resurrect people's relationships with invisible friends. Do you have any idea of how many children have friendships with invisible friends? Children are generally more postmodern than adults in that they have a stronger appreciation of the multi-storied nature of personhood. Just ask around. Ask children, or ask some of your adult relatives or friends about whether they had invisible friends in childhood. You will be surprised at the prevalence of these friendships. And do you have any idea of what a difference friendships with invisible friends make to children's lives?

Ken: It's not something that I think a whole lot about.

Michael: Neither did I, but some years ago, in response to a conversation with Cheryl White about invisible friends, I began to ask people questions about this. As Cheryl had predicted, I was surprised by the responses I received.

Ken: I guess that they provide support and reassurance; cure loneliness, and so on.

Michael: You can also pass the buck to them when things get tough. And invisible friends do more than all these things. They are very empathic and compassionate, and are prepared to go through all manner of experiences with children, even to join children in suffering. I am sure that you have heard of children getting a great deal of solace from being joined in illness by invisible friends. Invisible friends make it so much easier for children to take the things that they have to take. And children can tell invisible friends secrets and, in so doing, give themselves a voice in this adult world where there is so little space given to children's voices.

Ken: I'm reminded of a popular comic strip here in the United States, *Calvin and Hobbes* – about a boy, Calvin, who is about six or seven years old, and his stuffed tiger, Hobbes, who is quite animated and lively, and plays a significant part in Calvin's life. How do you connect these ideas to your work on helping people revise their relationship with the voices heard in schizophrenia?

Michael: In this culture, at a certain point, children get talked out of their relationship with their invisible friends. This is considered to be developmentally-appropriate. However, I do keep in mind that there are many cultures in which a person's relationship with the equivalent of invisible friends is preserved, and in which their ongoing contribution to the person's life is acknowledged.

In my work with people who are harassed by the voices of schizophrenia, I sometimes learn of a childhood relationship with an invisible friend. I can then ask these people questions about what these invisible friends meant to them, about how these invisible friends contributed to their lives in ways that were sustaining, about the circumstances of the loss of this relationship, and so on. I can ask people questions about what they think it was that they brought to the invisible friend's life, and to speculate about what the separation meant to the invisible friend. We can then explore the possibilities for reunion, and talk about how such a reunion might be empowering to both parties.

And then we can put together plans for the reunion. I have attended many such reunions, and have found them to be very moving and "warming" occasions.

Following these reunions, people can get their heads together with their invisible friends and document the hostile voices' usual habits of speech and action, develop predictions in regard to future attempts of these voices to establish supremacy, work on plans for how they might respond to this as a team, and so on.

Ken: Sounds fascinating! Although we have been mostly focussed on schizophrenia, I can see how these ideas have relevance to many other so-called psychiatric disorders.

Michael: They do. For example, take persons who are diagnosed with bipolar depression. We can engage these persons in externalizing conversations that have the effect of deconstructing both the grandiose ideas and the voice of depression. In the process, these people experience a degree of alienation in relation to these ideas and these voices, find that they are more able to monitor their emotional status, develop early intervention skills in reclaiming their lives from the destabilising effects of these ideas and voices, and become less vulnerable to acute episodes. But this is another story.

Ken: In the original interview I asked you about your theory on health/normality. In response, you said:

> *I think that all theories of health and normality are somewhat problematic because, regardless of their origins, they all wind up specifying lives and relationships, and all are entered into, albeit mostly inadvertently, in the service of subjugation. It is not possible to have a theory of normality without a positivist view and a utopian notion, and I do not believe that this can be sustained. A brief reflection on the history of ideas of health/normality is very discouraging of these ideas.*

So the work that you are talking about stands outside of most of the established conceptions of health and normality?

Michael: I believe that it does. But in some ways it is very helpful for us to know what the ideas and the practices of these notions of health and normality are. Upon identifying and clarifying these ideas and these practices, as well as the purposes to which they are put, people find themselves in a better position to determine possibilities for resisting what these notions incite them to do to their lives.

This knowledge also makes it possible for us to join with people in an exploration of those aspects of their life that they might be able to appreciate but that don't fit with these notions of health and normality. As some of these aspects become more visible to people, and as they become more embracing of these aspects, they are more able to honour their refusal to subject their lives to the ideas and practices that are informed by dominant notions of health and normality.

Ken: What is so important about the identification of and the honouring of this refusal?

Michael: Many of the people whom I meet who have a history of "schizophrenia" perceive themselves to have failed rather spectacularly in their attempts to be a person; that is, in their attempts to approximate the ways of being that are informed by dominant notions of health and normality. Other people in the community perceive this to constitute failure as well and thus contribute to the sense of otherness and the marginalisation that is so keenly experienced by people who have histories of "schizophrenia", "manic depressive illness", and so on.

In response to all of this, many people who have psychiatric diagnoses wind up missing out on the small grant of moral worth that is accorded to others in our communities, and, as well, they give themselves a particularly hard time over not "making it". As if this isn't stressful enough, they so often go on to subject themselves to a great deal of pressure in their attempts to craft their life according to what these notions of health and normality specify. They wind up perpetually "stretched". These are the sort of circumstances that are favourable to acute episodes.

Ken: In some ways, we all get caught up in evaluating our lives on healthy/sick, normal/abnormal continuums.

Michael: Yes. But many of us have a much greater chance of approximating those ways of being that are defined as healthy and normal than do others. Many of us are relatively successful at torturing ourselves into a state of "authenticity" and, in so doing, reproducing the "individuality" that is so venerated in this culture – although we all secretly know that we are not quite as together in regard to all of this as we appear to be to the world. But, psychotic expressions present an anathema to those cultural ways of being that we refer to as "self-possessed", "self-contained", "self-actualised", and so on. Psychotic experience, in this culture, rules people out of contention in the stakes for the achievement of personhood.

Ken: So you have talked about working with people in the honouring of the aspects of their life that they can appreciate and that don't fit with the dominant notions of health and normality. You have also talked about the importance of interpreting these aspects in ways that make it possible for them to be read as forms of refusal or as acts of resistance. Does this reopen the "stakes for personhood" as you would say it?

Michael: Yes it does. Stakes in the achievement of alternative versions of what it means to be a person.

Ken: Do externalizing conversations come into this?

Michael: They do. For example, the various ideas and practices that are associated with dominant notions of health and normality can be externalized as "expectations" and "ambitions". The requirements of these expectations and ambitions, their various incitements, and, as well, the terms that they dictate for people's lives, can be explored. This enables people to separate their lives and their identities from these ideas and practices, and opens space for what had previously been interpreted as failure to be reinterpreted as resistance or protest. In breaking their lives from those ways of being that are informed by dominant notions of health and normality, people experience a freedom to explore other ways of being in the world.

Ken: Having this kind of freedom to explore other ways of being would probably reduce a lot of stress in these people's lives – and maybe even their vulnerability to future acute episodes.

Michael: Very significantly.

Ken: These externalizing conversations are generated through a process of questioning?

Michael: Yes. This questioning process is maintained throughout this work, even in relation to those events that people read as progress. For example: *Are you doing this at a pace that suits the expectations, or at a pace that suits you?*

Ken: In *Narrative means to therapeutic ends,* you and David Epston provided many examples of therapeutic letters and other documents that assist people to re-author their lives according to preferred stories. Do you use letters and documents in this work as well?

Michael: Most certainly. In times of stress – when we find ourselves under significant duress when facing situations of adversity – we are all vulnerable to being separated from our knowledgeableness. At these times, we often experience a dearth of creative responses to the situations we find ourselves in; our usual problem-solving skills don't seem available to us, and our options for action seem to evaporate. Our focus of attention can become very narrow, we can begin to lose our sense of identity and, at times, when the stress that we are subject to is particularly acute, we can undergo something akin to paralysis.

Now, those people who have experienced psychotic episodes are ever so much more vulnerable to being dispossessed of their knowledgeableness and their preferred sense of identity at such times. And it is this dispossession that sets the scene for the experience of great personal insecurity and distress, and for further acute episodes. So it makes a great deal of sense for these people to carry with them, at all times, documents of their identity. These are documents that they can consult under those circumstances when they are losing sight of their knowledgeableness, when their sense of identity is at risk.

Ken: What do these documents look like?

Michael: There are many aspects to these documents, and many possible forms. Such documents can include some historical account of the person's ability to intervene, on his or her own behalf, in his/her own life. This is an account of personal agency, an account that emphasises what could be called the person's "agentive self". It includes details about what the person has been up against in the performance of this personal agency, and, against this background, emphasises the significance of any more recent steps that the person has been taking toward having more to say about how their life goes.

These documents are grounded in hope; for example, they often include details about the sort of personal qualities and other characteristics that were available to the person in the earlier years of their life, and speculation about how, when, and under what circumstances these might resurface in the service of the person's own plans and goals. These documents can also include details about any recent developments in the person's problem-solving skills.

Because other people's responses to the sort of identity claims that are reflected in these documents are of critical importance, those people who might provide an appropriate audience to this alternative account of the person's identity are specifically referred to in these documents. This is achieved in a way that is less likely to leave the response of this audience to chance – the wording is put in such a way as to invite acknowledging responses from this audience.

These documents are ever available to the person to consult, and are particularly valuable to them at times of stress and during crises. These are the times at which the person concerned is at risk of being dispossessed of their knowledgeableness. To facilitate this consultation, these documents usually include a self-referencing paragraph, one that further disempowers the voices through exposé, and one that invites the person to respond to crises with further revisions of their relationships with their voices. But this is not all, and perhaps I could here include an example of one of these documents.

Bev gave permission for this document to be reproduced here on the understanding that this might contribute to possibilities for others who experience voices. As she would be interested in feedback about whether this turned out to be the case, if appropriate, readers of this transcript might consider writing to her, c/-Dulwich Centre.

This document of identity was shaped by Bev's requirements, and they do not always take this form – for example, they can be set out in a series of points.

Ken: You said that these documents are always available for consultation?

Michael: Yes. It is not uncommon for the people who consult me to carry several documents of this sort on their person at all times. This way, they are ever available to be consulted. This considerably alleviates people's anxiety in the face of the trials and tribulations of everyday existence, and renders them less vulnerable to acute episodes.

Ken: It seems that a lot of the ideas and practices that you are talking about here would really help reduce the possibility that people will think of themselves as failures. They have on-hand written proof of an alternative story of their lives. Still, I wonder what happens when they are in such an acute crisis that hospitalisation is needed. What then?

Michael: You are right about the emphasis that I place on reducing the possibility that people will perceive themselves as failures. In our culture, the opportunities to experience failure are boundless and are ever-available. And, as already discussed, some people are more vulnerable to this than others and, for them, the experience of failure very significantly increases their vulnerability to what is often referred to as relapses. This has devastating consequences to their quality of life and to their course in life generally.

In the light of this, it makes sense for us to make it our business to ensure that the contexts of our work are structured to reduce the possibility that people might read failure into their responses to the world. This should be as true for the context of hospitalisation as it is for any other context. Unfortunately, however, the receiving frame that is in place for most admissions to psychiatric hospitals is one that reads the events that precipitate hospitalisation as regress. People are admitted as a

Document of Bev's Identity

In the past week, in the face of great odds, Bev was able to hang in, and, in confronting a great challenge, she found the resources to rise to the occasion. In this way she eventually got the upper hand, and reclaimed the territory of her own life. For passing this significant test, Bev gave herself six out of ten, Michael gave her seven out of ten, and Rosie gave her seven out of ten (Bev had requested this assessment).

Upon reflecting on this achievement to determine what sort of personal qualities Bev was depending upon, those of PATIENCE and STRENGTH came immediately to mind. These qualities have been available to Bev historically, and she has relied upon them to see her though difficult times. The fact that they are resurfacing now is cause for celebration.

There were other qualities that were available to Bev historically, and these include FORTITUDE, COURAGE, RESILIENCE, and STAMINA. It could be expected that these will also resurface and that Bev will be able to put them to work in further challenges to the fake authority of the voices. All of the qualities mentioned so far would be appreciated by Bev's mother, father, and two sisters.

In addition to this, recent events suggest the development of some entirely new personal skills. These are in the area of REACHING OUT, SELF-APPRECIATION, and SELF-EMBRACING. Bev's mother and her sisters would be delighted with this news, and would recognise the significance of this personal achievement.

There are developments that also suggest that Bev is breaking from the grief that she has held for so long in relation to her father's death. This is significant because she realises that her father's image should be important, but that it should not dominate her life.

Because the truth is very disempowering of hostile voices, whenever they try to hassle Bev she will read this document to them. This will confront them with their deceit and the petty nature of their claims, and will provoke them to take a back seat in her life.

result of having "breaks", because they are "decompensating", and so on. Upon admission to hospital, the events of people's lives are interpreted in ways that give rise to mostly negative connotations. To interpret the crises that precipitate admission to hospital as regress contributes significantly to despair, demoralisation and, of course, to distress – for those people who are being admitted, and for those who are in family, kinship, and friendship networks. Relatives and friends often experience feelings of inadequacy over not having "done better" in supporting the person who is admitted to hospital, and it is not at all unusual for them to experience substantial guilt at these times. As well, the negative connotations that are associated with hospital admission fuel, for everybody concerned, a sense of hopelessness about the future, and a personal dread that is based on predictions about the draining nature of the experiences that they have ahead of them in their relationship with the person who is being admitted. So, interpreting the crises that precipitate admission as regressive has profoundly negative effects on the lives and the relationships of all concerned.

Ken: But in proposing an alternative story about admission to the hospital, you are not suggesting that hospitalisation be understood as something to celebrate, are you?

Michael: No, definitely not. And at these times of crises it is important that people's distress be appropriately acknowledged. But I believe that the sense of failure, and the associated experiences of despair and demoralisation that are so often the outcome of these sort of admissions to hospital, are far from inevitable. In fact I believe that these experiences are mostly avoidable. We can establish different receiving frames for these admissions, ones that inform alternative interpretations of the crises that precipitate admission, ones that shape more positive outcomes for all involved – ones that undermine the possibilities for people to experience despair, demoralisation and a sense of failure under these circumstances.

So, it turns out that while people's experiences of distress associated with the events leading up to hospitalisation, and over the hospitalisation itself, can be powerfully acknowledged, the meanings associated with such admissions are open to negotiation. In fact, regardless of the situation, these meanings are always negotiated, and the particular meanings that are derived from this have an entirely significant effect on the outcome.

Ken: What is an example of one of these alternative receiving frames that you are referring to?

Michael: The "rite of passage" metaphor provides such a frame.[1] My understanding of this metaphor is derived from the work of the anthropologists van Gennep (1960) and Turner (1969). According to this work, there are three phases to the rites of passage that facilitate transitions in life. These are the "separation" phase, the "liminal" or "betwixt-and-between" phase, and the "reincorporation" phase.

I don't believe that this is the place to review in detail the work of these anthropologists, which is mostly about the structures that facilitate transitions in people's lives in traditional cultures. So, I will restrict myself to just a few comments about their rite of passage metaphor.

According to this metaphor, the first phase of a rite of passage facilitates, through communal ritual process, a novice's separation or detachment from a particular status and location in the social order – or, if you like, from a particular "state" of life. In the second phase, the novice enters a space that is between known worlds, one in which nothing is as it was, one that features a primary condition of ambiguity, one in which considerable confusion and disorientation are to be experienced. Everything that the novice had previously taken for granted can no longer be taken so. Then, after a period of time, it is deemed that the novice is ready to rejoin the familiar world, but at a different location in the social order, one that brings with it new responsibilities and freedoms, new habits of thought and action. This is the reincorporation phase, and in traditional cultures it is marked by community acknowledgement through ceremony. The novice is a novice no longer, and has arrived at a position in life that was not available to them beforehand. Communal acknowledgement plays an entirely significant role in the confirmation of, and authentication of, the new identity claims that are associated with reincorporation.

If we were to take this metaphor as a receiving frame for hospitalisation, then admission would be renamed discharge, and discharge would be renamed admission. At the point of hospitalisation it can be assumed that the person is being discharged from a particular status or location in the social world that was no longer appropriate for them to occupy, and this would inform a series of questions about what the person might be separating from in terms of expectations, roles, responsibilities, duties, obligations, habits of thought and action, affiliations, particular circumstances or conditions of life, etc. – that, for whatever reason, are no longer appropriate or acceptable. As stress is a significant feature in the precipitation of acute episodes, then many of these questions can be oriented to the identification of what might have been stressing of the person's life, of what had been stretching them beyond what was appropriate for them.

Questions of the sort that I am referring to here can be addressed at a meeting of family and friends around the time of admission. At times, the person who is undergoing the acute crisis is not able to be "present" for such a meeting, and in these circumstances the speculative responses to these questions can be checked out with the person at the point at which they become more "available".

Ken: I would guess that the rite of passage metaphor as you use it here could make a significant difference in the way that people might understand their hospitalisation and "inpatient" phase.

Michael: This metaphor provides for a reinterpretation of the confusion and disorientation that is almost routinely experienced by people at these times of crisis, for it proposes that the "inpatient" phase is a liminal or betwixt-and-between phase. People can come to an appreciation of the fact that there is always some distance between the point of separation from something, and the point of arrival at something else, and that in this space it is only reasonable to expect a very considerable degree of confusion and disorientation. Within the context of this receiving frame, these experiences cease to be read as regress, but as the virtual inevitable outcome of journeying to a new place in life.

To facilitate this reading of experience during the period of admission, staff can spend time with the person and members of his/her kinship and friendship networks over (a) further speculation about what the person might be separating from, (b) what circumstances of life might be more suitable for him/her and more favourable to quality of life, and (c) the investigation of any clues that might provide some thoughts about the ways of life that might be available for the person to step into at the completion of this particular transition.

Ken: And I suppose that the discharge from hospital would be the "reincorporation phase"?

Michael: Yes. Family, friends, acquaintances, staff, and so on, can be invited to another gathering which is described as the re-admission meeting. At this meeting, an opportunity is provided for the person to speak as an authority on their own life and to give an account of their journey, one that includes information about what this has clarified for them in regard to the circumstances of life that would favour quality of life, and that would suit them better personally. In this context, the others who are present are encouraged to respond in ways that are acknowledging of the person's status as an authority on his/her life, of the person's knowledgeableness. As well, all of those present at these gatherings are encouraged to explore any alterations that might be necessary in their relationships to the person in order to accommodate these changes.

Ken: How does this affect the course of hospitalisations that many people are going through?

Michael: On those occasions that I have been able to structure this sort of receiving context, which is nowhere near as often as I would have liked, it has definitely had the effect of reducing the length and number of hospital admissions. But the sample is small, and I have not had the opportunity to follow this up further in recent years.

What is most important about establishing this alternative receiving frame is that people learn to read their experiences of distress and confusion differently. And this even makes it possible for them to respond differently to their milder experiences of psychotic phenomena – those that do not precipitate hospitalisation. These experiences come to signify a liminal phase that opens the possibility for people to take further steps to determine a lifestyle that would suit them. This very significantly undermines the despair, insecurity, and panic, which are all complicating in the sense that they intensify the psychotic experience. In the place of this despair, insecurity, and panic, we see the development of a certain sense of curiosity about the outcome of the transition, and of the sort of hope that helps people through these crises.

Ken: What about future hospitalisations? Would they tend to undermine the validity of this rite of passage metaphor?

Michael: Not if these are predicted, which they reasonably can be. The idea that life is comprised of a series of transitions is not at all novel in our culture. And it can be openly assumed that the people who have experienced hospitalisation in a context that is informed by the rite of passage metaphor are likely to go through further transitions marked by the phases of separation, liminality and reincorporation. And if the circumstances of these hospitalisations are favourable, this turns out to be not such a bad context for the negotiation of these liminal phases of a person's life.

So, when people have a history of many and frequent admissions, at times it makes lots of sense to sit down and talk with them about the wisdom of scheduling future admissions in advance of psychotic episodes. This scheduling can be determined by reviewing previous admissions to determine the average time elapsed between admissions, and by bringing the scheduled admission ahead of this by a slim margin.

Ken: So, what happens during these subsequent admissions? How are they structured?

Michael: In exactly the same way as those we have already discussed. The admission is seen as an opportunity to take time out to review one's life to determine which aspects of it might be incompatible with those ways of life that the person is most suited to. This provides for people the opportunity to identify what circumstances of life might be stressing of them, and which of these circumstances they might be ready to break their lives from.

Ken: So this doesn't mean that the person winds up being hospitalised more often?

Michael: The therapeutic practices that we have been reviewing throughout this interview all have the potential to reduce admissions to hospital. And this is no less true for the practice of scheduled admissions that I am describing. The sort of admissions that I am proposing actually work against acute episodes. And, as people experience fewer disabling episodes, they begin to modify the schedule by reducing the length of admissions and by stretching the interval between admissions.

Ken: How realistic is it to believe that institutions like psychiatric hospitals are going to be interested and able to do what amounts to turning their procedures upside down?

Michael: I think that the potential to achieve this is significant. There are many administrators and clinical directors out there who are looking for some viable alternatives to the established practices of hospitalisation, alternatives that are likely to contribute to the quality of life of the people who are the recipients of their services, and alternatives that are likely to deal with the high levels of malaise and demoralisation experienced by the staff of these institutions.

Ken: In this country [USA] insurance companies are having a lot more to say about treatment generally, including hospital admissions and the length of admissions. What happens to the possibilities to practice what you are suggesting under such circumstances?

Michael: I don't really know enough about the "ins" and the "outs" of what is happening here to comment much. Obviously what I am proposing here could be as much in the interests of insurance companies as it is in everybody else's interest. But I don't know how well wisdom sits with insurance companies.

Ken: Throughout this interview, your responses to my questions have conveyed a strong sense of the possibilities that are available to mental health professionals in this work. But what are the options for mental health professionals who want to take up the sort of possibilities that you have outlined in this interview, but who do not have the backing of their institutions, and who are not in positions of significant power?

Michael: Rarely do the institutions of our culture succeed in establishing states of pure domination. Because of this, in most institutions, spaces or gaps can be found through which workers can express their moral agency. And, in stepping into these gaps, we can all play a role in the transformation of the institutions that we work for.

We can ignore the arbitrary boundaries of these institutions, and we can go out and meet with people and encourage them to draw distinctions around which ways of speaking about their lives are respectful and honouring of their knowledges, and which ways of speaking about their lives are marginalising and disqualifying of this knowledgeableness. We can join with people in developing ideas for informing the institutions of this, and for recruiting the active participation of these institutions in the further development of practices that these people consider more personally empowering. I have seen those people who are the "consumers" of psychiatric services enter into this educative role with a great deal of benevolence and empathy for the staff of the institutions concerned.

Ken: This has been rather a long interview, and perhaps we should draw it to a close. Would you like to make some parting comments?

Michael: Yes. Despite the length of this interview, what we have been talking about is a partial account of this work. There are many other considerations.

Ken: Any that you would like to briefly name here.

Michael: Yes. The provision of appropriate community support to people with psychiatric diagnoses is a consideration of critical importance. For those readers who want to review this dimension, and who haven't yet begun, I would suggest consulting Chris Beels' "Invisible village" (1989). It is a great starting point.

Ken: I've really enjoyed this interview, Michael. I think a lot of what you have said really challenges the ways in which so-called psychiatric patients have been labelled, shunned, categorised, written-off, and otherwise marginalised, or, in your own words, subjugated – and the use of this term gives the whole process a more political flavour – which is what you have so refreshingly brought to our attention. Thank you.

Michael: And I've enjoyed this opportunity to renew my contact with you, and to further discuss this work.

Note

1. This metaphor has been employed by others for similar purposes in modifying the receiving frames for admission to residential care facilities (see Menses & Durrant 1986).

References

Beels, C. C. (1989). The invisible village. In C. C. Beels & L. L. Bachrach (Eds.), Survival strategies for public psychiatry [Special issue]. *New Directions for Mental Health Services*, (42), 27–40.

Menses, G., & Durrant, M. (1986). Contextual residential care. *Dulwich Centre Review*, pp. 3-14.

Turner, V. (1969). *The ritual process; Structure and anti-structure*. New York, NY: Cornell University Press.

van Gennep, A. (1960). *The rites of passage*. Chicago, IL: University of Chicago Press.

chapter three

Saying hullo again:
The incorporation of the lost
relationship in the resolution of grief

by Michael White

> *Freud ... suggests that the completion of the mourning process requires that those left behind develop a new reality which no longer includes what has been lost. But ... it must be added that full recovery from mourning may restore what has been lost, maintaining it through incorporation into the present. Full recollection and retention may be as vital to recovery and wellbeing as forfeiting memories.* (Myerhoff, 1982, p. 111)

For some time I have been exploring the 'saying hullo' metaphor and its application to grief work. This exploration has been prompted by particular experiences in therapy with persons who have been diagnosed elsewhere as suffering from 'delayed grief' or 'pathological mourning'. Many of these persons have received intensive and lengthy treatments that have been oriented by the normative model of the grief process, or by the chemical approach to life's problems.

I usually find that such persons are well acquainted with the grief map and can locate their experience in relation to it. They clearly understand that they have failed, in their grief work, to reach the appropriate destination. They 'know' that their arrival at this destination will be evidenced by a fully experienced 'goodbye', acceptance of the permanence of the loss of the loved one, and a desire to get on with a new life that is disconnected from that person.

At first contact, persons experiencing 'delayed grief' or 'pathological mourning' look as if they have lost their own 'selves' as well as the loved one. Without prompting, they put therapists in touch with their loss and its subsequent effect on their life, freely relating the details of their sense of emptiness, worthlessness, and feelings of depression. Such is their despair that I have often felt quite overwhelmed at the outset of therapy. Although I commonly discern invitations from these persons to join in further 'more of the same' conversations that are activated by the 'saying goodbye' metaphor, I am usually able to decline these.

It can be expected that, under these circumstances, persisting with 'grief work' oriented by the normative model will complicate the situation further, rather than empower these persons and enrich their lives. Such is the desolation that these persons experience, establishing a context in therapy for the incorporation of the lost relationship seems far more strongly indicated than further efforts at encouraging the forfeiture of this relationship. My investigation of the 'saying hullo' metaphor was prompted by this consideration.

Guided by this metaphor, I formulated and introduced questions that I hoped would open up the possibility for persons to reclaim their relationship with the lost loved one. Surprised by the effect of these questions in the resolution of the sense of emptiness and feelings of depression, I decided to explore the metaphor further. I expected that a fuller understanding of the processes involved would enable me to more effectively assist persons in the re-positioning of themselves in relation to the death of a loved one, a re-positioning that would bring the relief so strongly desired.

Mary

Mary was forty-three years old when she sought help for what she described as 'unresolved loss'. Some six years earlier, her husband, Ron, had died suddenly from heart failure. This had been entirely unexpected. Until that time, everything had been fine for Mary. She and Ron had enjoyed a 'rich and loving' friendship, one that they both valued very highly.

Upon Ron's death, Mary's world fell apart. Grief-stricken, and feeling 'numbed' from that time, she 'simply went through the motions of life', not experiencing consolation from any quarter. Her numbness survived a number of attempts to 'work through' her grief via counselling. Medication had not provided relief. Despite this, Mary persisted in her attempts to achieve some sense of wellbeing by consulting therapists and 'working on acceptance' over the next five years.

At my first meeting with Mary, she said that she had all but given up hope that she would ever regain even a semblance of wellbeing. She thought she would never be able to say goodbye. After Mary had put me in touch with her despair, I invited her to escape the 'deadly serious' consequences of Ron's death.

I wondered aloud whether saying goodbye was a helpful idea anyway, and about whether it might be a better idea to say hullo to Ron. Further, I said that the desolation she so keenly experienced might mean that she had said goodbye just too well. Mary's response was one of puzzlement and surprise. Had she heard what she thought she had? I repeated my thoughts and saw, for the first time, a spark in her.

I then asked if she would be interested in experimenting with saying hullo to Ron or if she thought he was buried too deep for her to entertain this idea. Mary began to sob; easy sobbing, not desperate. I waited. After ten or fifteen minutes she suddenly said: 'Yes, he's been buried too deep for me'. She smiled and then said that it might be helpful to 'dig him up a bit'. So I began to ask some questions:[1]

- *If you were seeing yourself through Ron's eyes right now, what would you be noticing about yourself that you could appreciate?*
- *What difference would it make to how you feel if you were appreciating this in yourself right now?*
- *What do you know about yourself that you are awakened to when you bring alive the enjoyable things that Ron knew about you?*
- *What difference would it make to you if you kept this realisation, about yourself, alive on a day-to-day basis?*
- *What difference would feeling this way make to the steps that you could take to get back into life?*

- *How could you let others know that you have reclaimed some of the discoveries about yourself that were clearly visible to Ron, and that you personally find attractive?*

- *How would being aware of that which has not been visible to you for the past six years enable you to intervene in your life?*

- *What difference will knowing what you now know about yourself make to your next step?*

- *In taking this next step, what else do you think you might find out about yourself that could be important for you to know?*

Mary struggled with these questions through alternating bursts of sadness and joy. Over the two subsequent sessions she shared with me the important rediscoveries that she was making about herself and life. At follow-up, some twelve months later, Mary said: 'It's strange, but when I discovered that Ron didn't have to die for me, that I didn't have to separate from him, I became less preoccupied with him and life was richer'.

John

John was thirty-nine years old when he consulted me about longstanding 'difficulties with self-esteem'. He couldn't recall not having a critical attitude toward himself. Throughout his life he had hungered for approval and recognition from others. For this, he hated himself all the more, believing that he lacked substance as a person and that this was clearly apparent to others.

John considered himself loved by his wife and children and believed that his experience in this family of procreation had gone some way toward countering his nagging self-doubt – but never far enough. His self-doubt was so easily triggered by what he considered to be the most trivial of circumstances. He had, on various occasions, sought professional advice, but had not experienced the relief that he was seeking.

In view of the long history of John's self-rejection, I asked for further details about his life. He told me that, as far as he knew, he had a happy childhood until the death of his mother at the tender age of seven, just before his eighth birthday. No-one in the family had coped with this at all well and, for a time, John's father had been a lost person to everyone, including himself. John had vivid recall of the events surrounding his mother's death. He experienced disbelief for some considerable time, always expecting that she would show up around the next corner. He then became entirely heartbroken. Eventually his father re-married to a caring person 'but things were never really the same again'.

I asked John about what difference it would have made to how he felt about himself now if things had remained the same – if his mother hadn't died. At this point he began to get tearful. Didn't he think she might have gone missing from his life for too long? Was it really helpful for her to remain absent from his life? He looked surprised. Would he mind if I asked more questions? 'No, that would be fine.' I proceeded with the following:

- *What did your mother see when she looked at you through her loving eyes?*
- *How did she know these things about you?*
- *What is it about you that told her about this?*
- *What can you now see in yourself that had been lost to you for many years?*
- *What difference would it make to your relationships with others if you carried this knowledge with you in your daily life?*
- *How would this make it easier for you to be your own person, rather than a person for others?*
- *What could you do to introduce others to this new picture of yourself as a person?*
- *How would bringing others into this new picture of your person enable you to nurture yourself more?*
- *In what way would such an experience of nurturing yourself affect your relationship with yourself?*

I met with John on three further occasions at two week intervals, and then for a follow-up eight months later. Over this time, he took various steps to keep his mother's 'picture' of him in circulation, and arrived at a new relationship with himself, one that was self-accepting rather than self-rejecting. He no longer felt vulnerable to those events that used to drive him into self-doubt.

Discussion

Experience of experience

• *If you were seeing yourself through Ron's eyes right now, what would you be noticing about yourself that you could appreciate?*

Those questions that seemed most helpful in assisting persons to reclaim these important relationships, were the ones that invited a recounting of what they perceived to be the deceased person's positive experience of them. This recounting was an expression of their experience of specific aspects of the deceased person's experience. These questions had an immediate and visible effect. The memories that they touched off were not just a factual account of historical events, but a full and vivid re-living of experience, one that incorporated the person's various senses and emotions.

It was clear that, in this recounting, a re-experience of past selves was triggered off. Various lost or forgotten knowledges of self seemed to become available for persons to express. How is this process to be understood?

In striving to make sense of our lives, we face the task of arranging our experiences of events in sequences across time in such a way as to arrive at a coherent account of ourselves. Specific experiences of events of the past and the present, and those that are predicted to occur in the future, are connected to develop this account, which has been referred to as a story or self-narrative:

> The past, present, and future are not only constructed but connected in a lineal sequence that is defined by systematic if not causal relations. How we depict any one segment is related to our conception of the whole, which I choose to think of as a story. (Bruner, 1986a, p. 141)

The success of this task provides us with a sense of continuity and meaning in our lives. We rely on this sense for the ordering of our daily lives and for the interpretation of further experiences. However, this sense is gained at a price. A narrative can never re-present the richness of what Bruner (1986) has called our 'lived experience':

> ... life experience is richer than discourse. Narrative structures organize and give meaning to experience, but there are always feelings and lived experience not fully encompassed by the dominant story. (Bruner, 1986a, p. 143)

The structuring of a narrative requires recourse to a selective process in which we prune, from our experience, those events that do not fit with the dominant evolving story that we and others have about us. Thus, over time, much of our stock of lived experience goes unstoried and is never 'told' or expressed.

However, under certain circumstances, it is possible for persons to re-live neglected aspects of their lived experience in un-edited form. At these times the sequential arrangement of events across time is temporarily undone and replaced by what Myerhoff (1982) refers to as 'simultaneity'. Thus, 'a sense of oneness with all that has been one's history is achieved' (p. 110).

I believe that those questions that invite persons to recount what they perceive to be the deceased person's experience of them achieve this simultaneity. In this reaching back into experience, alternative and previously lost knowledges can be located and re-performed. Thus, new and enriching acknowledgements and validations of self can become available to persons.

Selection of alternative knowledges

* *What do you know about yourself that you are awakened to when you bring alive the enjoyable things that Ron knew about you?*

In encouraging persons to claim the alternative knowledges that become available in this reliving of experience, I have found other questions to be helpful. These questions invite persons to review this experience and to locate those alternative knowledges of self that present the 'facts' about self that are most appealing; those 'facts' that will assist them and others to 'write' a new story of their lives.

These questions also assist persons in the development of an awareness that:

Every telling is an arbitrary imposition of meaning on the flow of memory, in that we highlight some causes and discount others; that is, every telling is interpretive. (Bruner, 1986b, p. 7)

Circulation of self-knowledge

* *How could you let others know that you have reclaimed some of the discoveries about yourself that were clearly visible to Ron, and that you find personally attractive?*

As 'self' is a performed self, the survival of alternative knowledges is enhanced if the new ideas and new meanings that they bring forth are put into circulation: 'The hard-won meanings should be said, painted, danced, dramatised, put into circulation' (Turner, 1986, p. 37).

To achieve this circulation, an audience to the performance of such new meanings is required. Questions can be derived that identify and recruit this audience. In the 'reading' of these new meanings, this audience participates, via feedback, in new productions of the person's self. The production of self is a recursive process, one in which selected aspects of one's experience are performed, and in which this very performance contributes to the stock of one's experience of events from which self-knowledge is derived.

Consciousness of production of productions

* *What difference will knowing what you now know about yourself make to your next step?*
* *In taking this next step, what else do you think you might find out about yourself that could be important for you to know?*

Further questions can be introduced that encourage persons to entertain, more fully, their role in the production of their own productions of self. Consciousness of one's production of one's productions opens new possibilities for persons to direct their own course in life.

As persons become aware of the process in which they are both a performer in, and audience to, their own performances, new choices become available to them in regard to the alternative knowledges of self that they might co-operate with – and they experiences themselves as 'the authors of themselves' (Myerhoff, 1986, p. 263).

Other applications

Loss of young child

Parents who have lost very young children have found the 'saying hullo' metaphor helpful, including in the circumstances of the death of unborn children. After being introduced to the idea, they do not experience great difficulty in speculating about what the child's experience of them, as parents, might have been, and then incorporating this.

Child abuse

The applicability of this metaphor has also been explored and found to be helpful with children who have been 'taken into care' with histories of being repeatedly and seriously abused. As a result of such abuse, these children usually relate to their self with hate, and go about doing their best to fail, often mutilating their own lives and futures through destructive behaviour.

In these circumstances, I have worked with the child and residential care workers to locate 'unique outcomes' (White, 1988) that identify occurrences of adult persons relating positively and helpfully to the child, instead of negatively and harmfully. These unique outcomes can be located historically and/or currently. For example, it might be discovered that a certain school teacher had taken a particularly kindly attitude towards the child, that a community worker had taken a special interest in the child's plight, or that a residential care worker has recently made some important and pleasing observations about the child.

Once unique outcomes have been established, questions can be introduced that invite the child to render them significant through a performance of meaning. These questions encourage speculation about the alternative knowledges of self that are associated with the unique outcomes. Examples of these questions follow:

- *What do you think it is that your teacher noticed about you that your …* [the abusing adult] *was blind to?*

- *What is it about you that told your teacher this?*

- *So what did this teacher know about you that you can know about yourself?*

- *If* [the abusing adult] *had not been so blind to these facts, and had not missed out on you as a person, what difference would this have made to their attitude towards you?*

These questions, and those that encourage the circulation of the alternative knowledges and a consciousness of the production of one's productions, undermine the child's self-hate and their participation in the mutilation of their own lives and futures.

Adult self-abuse

I have introduced a variation of this work to women and men who, as a result of emotional and/or physical abuse during childhood and adolescence, maintain a very negative and rejecting attitude towards themselves in adult life. This self-rejection is the outcome of their incorporation of the abusing adult/s' attitude towards them.

These persons cannot rest. They feel perpetually compelled to operate upon and discipline their self according to the abuser's attitudes. They are unable to trust any of the more personally favourable versions of their self that they might encounter through life.

It is helpful to invite these persons to attend to those unique outcomes that identify recent occasions during which they were able to treat themselves with a fraction of 'self-acceptance', or occasions during which they protested their submission to the dominant specifications of self that were established by the abuser.

Once a unique outcome has been identified, questions can be introduced that encourage a specific recounting of childhood and adolescent experiences, one that locates similar but historical episodes of self-acceptance or protest. Efforts are also made to pinpoint the person's age at the time of these historical episodes. Further questions are then helpful in assisting these persons to revise their relationship with their self:

- *If you were looking at yourself through the eyes of that ten-year-old boy right now, what would he be seeing in you that he would really appreciate?*
- *What is it about the development of you as a person that would be most important to him?*
- *Noticing this, would he encourage you to try to be someone else, or would he take you for who you are?*
- *Why do you think he would have liked you for a parent?*
- *What difference do you think it would have made to his life if he'd had you for a parent?*
- *What could you do to side with this ten-year-old boy's attitude towards you, rather than … [the abusing adult's] attitude?*
- *What difference would this make in your relationship with yourself, to how you would treat yourself?*

The responses to these questions contribute to the reclaiming of, and to the performance of, alternative self-knowledges, and to the forging of a new relationship with self through an experience of 'self-specification'.

Separation

The 'saying hullo' metaphor is also appropriate in circumstances where there has been a loss of a relationship that has not been incurred by death. Often, such a loss is devastating to the person who did not initiate the separation and who wanted to persist with the relationship.

One common reaction is for these persons to feel betrayed by their partner, and to submit to extraordinary self-doubt. At times, this is associated with an intoxicating self-righteous anger. These responses usually relate to a new perception that they were never really loved by the other, but 'just strung along'. I refer to this new perception as the 'second story'.

When these responses persist, questions can be introduced that bring the 'first story' – the one that includes the experience of being a lovable person – out from the shadow of the second story; questions that invite the incorporation of the first story, and an active co-operation with it. Successful incorporation resolves the self-doubt and self-righteous anger.

Conclusion

Many persons who have consulted me over problems that relate to unresolved grief have found the 'saying hullo' metaphor, and the questions derived from this metaphor, to be helpful. I have consistently found that, through the incorporation of the lost relationship, those problems defined in terms such as 'pathological mourning' and 'delayed grief' are resolved. In achieving this incorporation, persons arrive at a new relationship with their self. Their attitude towards their self becomes a more accepting and embracing one, and they come to treat themselves with greater kindness and compassion.

The illustrations given in this paper provide some examples of the utilisation of this metaphor. However, these examples by no means exhaust the possible applications.

In focussing here on the 'saying hullo' metaphor, I am not taking a position against the utilisation of the saying goodbye metaphor. There is much to say goodbye to, including to a material reality and to hopes and expectations, etc. Instead, I believe that the process of grief is a 'saying goodbye and then saying hullo' phenomenon.

Having said this, I would argue that every experience of loss is unique, as are the requirements for the resolution of every loss. Any metaphor is only helpful to the extent that it recognises, and facilitates the expression of, this uniqueness, and doesn't subject persons to normative specifications.

Note

[1.] Of course, the examples of questions that are given in this paper are not presented by therapists in barrage-like fashion, but within the context of a co-evolving process. Each question is sensitively attuned to the person's response to the previous question.

References

Bruner, E. M. (1986a). Ethnography as narrative. In V. W. Turner & E. M. Bruner (Eds.), *The anthropology of experience* (pp. 139-155). Chicago, IL: University of Illinois Press.

Bruner, E. M. (1986b). Experience and its expressions. In V. W. Turner & E. M. Bruner (Eds.), *The anthropology of experience* (pp. 3-30). Chicago, IL: University of Illinois Press.

Myerhoff, B. (1982). Life history among the elderly: Performance, visibility and re-membering. In J. Ruby (Ed.), *A crack in the mirror: Reflexive perspectives in anthropology* (pp. 99-117). Philadelphia, PA: University of Pennsylvania Press.

Myerhoff, B. (1986). 'Life not death in Venice': Its second life. In V. W. Turner & E. M. Bruner (Eds.), *The anthropology of experience* (pp. 261-286). Chicago, IL: University of Illinois Press.

Turner, V. (1986). Dewey, Dilthey, and Drama: An essay in the anthropology of experience. In V. W. Turner & E. M. Bruner (Eds.), *The anthropology of experience* (pp. 33-44). Chicago, IL: University of Illinois Press.

White, M. (1988). The process of questioning: A therapy of literary merit? *Dulwich Centre Newsletter* (Winter), 8–14.

chapter four

Re-membering

by Michael White

The image of membered lives brings into play the metaphor of a 'club' – a club of life is evoked. This metaphor opens up options for the exploration of how a person's club of life is membered – of how this club of life is constituted through its membership, and of how the membership of this club is arranged in terms of rank or status. As well, this metaphor suggests unique possibilities for action in the form of re-membering practices, which inform a 'special type of recollection'. I will here quote Myerhoff (1982) on this subject:

> To signify this special type of recollection, the term 'Re-membering' may be used, calling attention to the reaggregation of members, the figures who belong to one's life story, one's own prior selves, as well as significant others who are part of the story. Re-membering, then, is a purposive, significant unification, quite different from the passive, continuous fragmentary flickerings of images and feelings that accompany other activities in the normal flow of consciousness. (p. 111)

This notion of re-membering, and the club metaphor, suggests possibilities for persons to engage in a revision of the membership of their club of life. This is an engagement that provides persons with the opportunity to have a greater say about the status of particular memberships of their club of life. Through re-membering practices, persons can suspend or elevate, revoke or privilege, and downgrade or upgrade specific memberships of their lives. Various classes of honorary membership can be established and bestowed, including life memberships. It is in this way, through re-membering practices, that persons can have more to say about whose voices are to be recognised on matters of their identity, and about who might be authorised to speak on such matters. And, apart from contributing to persons having a greater say about the status of the existing memberships of their club of life, re-membering practices also contribute to options in regard to the selection of new memberships from persons and groups of persons who might be available and willing to join – from persons and groups of persons who might be invited to take out preferred memberships in one's club of life.

This notion of re-membering also suggests possibilities and provides opportunities for persons to more directly acknowledge the important and valued contributions that others have made to their lives. When these opportunities are taken up into re-membering practices, these other persons generally experience this as significantly honouring of them. As well, in engaging in these acknowledgements of the contributions of others, one experiences one's own life being more richly described. Such acts of acknowledgement can also have persons re-activating dormant memberships through re-engaging with some of the figures of their history. In these acts, a person experiences the stories of their lives linked to the stories of the lives of others around particular themes and shared values and commitments. And, more than this, these practices of re-membering generally make it more possible for people to experience, in their day-to-day lives, the fuller presence of these figures, even when they are not available to be there in a material sense (for example, in the case of persons who have died or from whom a separation has occurred). The sense of being joined in this way, and of experiencing one's life more richly described, contributes to new possibilities for action in the world. It also renders persons less vulnerable to experiences of being alone in the face of adversity – it provides an antidote to a sense of isolation.

Through these re-membering practices, in the revision of the membership of a person's club of life, those memberships that are honoured or elevated in status can be considered to be those that have provided the context for the generation of the person's preferred knowledges of life and skills of living. These are frequently the historical associations that have been significant in the derivation of the person's preferred account of their identity. In reviewing these associations, those knowledges and skills, and those accounts of identity, can be identified and explored in their particularities – the significant discoveries, realisations, conclusions, learnings, problem-solving practices, and so on, become more thickly described. This contributes very significantly to a person's sense of being knowledged, to the shaping of new proposals for action in their lives, and to specific expressions of these proposals.

Before proceeding to review the relevance of re-membering practices to the work and to the lives of therapists, a diversion is warranted – one that provides an account of re-membering practices as they might be expressed in narrative work with persons who consult therapists. This diversion will take the form of a brief review of the history of re-membering practices in my work, and three stories of narrative practice, the first of which is principally a transcript. These stories are unique in the sense that the narratives of persons' lives always are – in the sense that every therapeutic journey evolves in ways that could not have been predicted ahead of the journey itself, and in the sense that each journey brings with it options for entering new territories of thought and practice. However, these three stories of narrative practice are not unique in regard to the general effects of re-membering practices – these practices invariably make a very significant contribution to lives being richly described, and to the development of a wide range of options for action in the social world.

Saying hullo again

About ten years ago I started to organise and to commit to paper some of the thoughts and practices that I had been exploring in working with people who were in 'trouble' with grief – persons who had been referred to me with diagnoses of 'delayed grief' and 'pathological mourning'. Twelve months later these thoughts were published as 'Saying hullo again: The reincorporation of the lost relationship in the resolution of grief' (White, 1988). The thoughts expressed in this paper contradicted the idea that working with grief is about assisting persons to go through the stages of a well-known journey so that they might arrive at an acceptance of the loss, and so that they might then proceed with their lives without the lost loved one.

The 'saying hullo again' paper spoke to some conclusions that I had reached in my meetings with persons who were seeking consultation over 'delayed grief' and 'pathological mourning': (a) these persons were already profoundly bereft; (b) this was a powerful testimony to the significance of, and the love experienced in, the lost relationship; (c) the loss of the loved one had contributed to wide gaps in the person's sense of identity; and (d) further work oriented by the known and established grief maps was counter-productive in addressing these losses. Too much had already gone from the lives of these persons – an experience of the voices of, and the touch of, the lost loved ones was already an achievement that was too elusive to these persons.

In response to these conclusions, I began to explore 'saying hullo again' conversations – conversations that were reincorporating of the person's relationship with the lost loved one, conversations that contributed to making available to persons, in their day-to-day lives, experiences of the touch and the voices of the lost loved ones.[1] Persons' responses to these conversations were dramatic – they broke from the desperation, from the despair, and from the sense of emptiness that had become the central experience of their lives, and reclaimed a familiar and comforting sense of identity. The 'saying hullo again' conversations that I discussed in this paper were in part oriented by what at the time I called 'experience of experience' questions, and which I now more regularly refer to as 're-membering questions'.

In providing here some account of the history of re-membering practices in my work, I thought it appropriate to briefly revisit these practices as they are expressed in the context of addressing profound grief in relation the death of a loved one.

Sophia and Bill

I first met Sophia fifteen years ago. At that time she was struggling with a pervasive depression and with an anorexia nervosa that was constantly threatening to deprive her of her life. This struggle wasn't new. Over many years this depression and anorexia nervosa had driven her into actions against her own life, and had precipitated admissions to hospital. Sophia was tiring of the struggle.

At first, Sophia was decidedly unenthusiastic about meeting with me and about pursuing yet another course of therapy. She had no confidence that this could lead to a good outcome, but had decided to go along with it for the sake of her partner, Bill. He had refused to be discouraged in his efforts to join with Sophia in search of a solution to the depression and the anorexia nervosa, and had remained steadfast in his belief that she would find a better life. Bill was a force for life.

Over the course of our meetings, Sophia identified, and gradually broke her life from, the voice of self-hate and the voice of anorexia nervosa. As she did so she began to explore and step into other accounts of her identity. Bill's contribution at this time was invaluable. He was ever ready to support Sophia in the meaning-making conversations that we were engaging in, and in the exploration of the proposals for action in her life that were informed by these conversations. And at no point in this work did he assume that he could have a voice for Sophia. As Sophia began to embrace life, Bill initiated a critical reflection on his ways of being in his relationship with her, and, as an outcome of this, took many steps to ensure that Sophia would be unhindered in this embrace. This was Sophia's chance, and for this Bill would move a mountain if this was necessary. Bill's presence in these conversations also warmed and sustained me.

For Sophia, her embrace of life was not a reclaiming of it. She believed that life had never been in her grasp. As part of what Sophia referred to as 'being born' as a person, she developed an interest in making small stuffed creatures. This she found to be life-giving, and it was through this project that she developed new connections with the outside world. As Sophia's life went forward, we had many causes to celebrate together. Through the next years I would hear from Sophia from time to time, sometimes a letter, sometimes a call – and in this way I was an audience to the many developments in her life, including her enrolment in a women's studies program. Bill's voice was always there in these developments too – always believing, always acknowledging.

I knew that Bill had decided to take early retirement in 1996. He and Sophia were looking forward to spending more time together, and had planned many adventures for this phase of their lives. Then suddenly, in early 1996, Bill died of heart failure. I was called by Sophia's general practitioner. She was in hospital, recovering from a major overdose – now off the critical list, but depressed and furious with him and the hospital staff for having saved her life. She had intended to kill herself, and was now assuring everybody that the only outcome of the medical intervention would be a brief reprieve. Sophia was determined to be successful in the next attempt on her life, and was asserting that the medical intervention had extended her life by a matter of weeks, not months or years. It was her desire to be six feet under the ground, lying alongside Bill. This was the only place that she wanted to be. During the telephone conversation, the general practitioner informed me that Sophia said that she would speak to me, but that she would be entirely intolerant of anyone's efforts to talk her out of her resolve to join Bill. Knowing Sophia and Bill as I did, I appreciated that this resolve was a testimony to the powerful love that they had for each other, and to the wonderful contribution that they had made to each other's life.

I visited the hospital, and sat with Sophia. She was indeed angry, and just so miserable. She talked flatly of her desolation and of the greyness that had enveloped her life, of the gift of being that had now been withdrawn, of the impossibility of proceeding in life without Bill, of the lost hopes that they'd had for his retirement, of her desire to be lying alongside him, and of her conviction that nothing could stop the inevitable – the medical intervention had saved her on this occasion, but it had only put off what was inevitable. Sophia also made it clear that she would not spend time with anyone who had an agenda of talking her out of her resolve to join Bill. I gave her my undertaking not to do this, but asked if it would be okay with her if we had some conversations about options that would enable her to again be with Bill, to experience his presence, but that did not require her to be six feet under the ground. This was acceptable to Sophia, and so began a series of conversations that were oriented by the 'saying hullo again' metaphor.

The following transcript is of an interview that took place nine weeks after Bill's death, and constituted one of the turning-points in our work. In this interview, Sophia had been talking of the advice that she had been receiving from many quarters – to grieve, to let go of Bill, to accept the loss, and to get on with her life. Sophia just knew that this 'common knowledge' was not right for her. We explored how it was that Sophia had been able to respect this conclusion, and discovered that she had achieved this by keeping faith with and relying upon her 'uncommon knowledge'.

Transcript[2]

It's a knowledge that seems like an uncommon knowledge in a way? Do you mean it's not a knowledge that everybody can relate to?

It just seems like everyone else, apart from a few close friends, think that it's time just to move forward and put everything else behind me.

Put this behind you and move forward – is what most other people seem to think this is all about?

[Sophia nods]

What are you thinking about right now?

I'm thinking about what Bill would think.

Yes. Can you tell me about what he would think?

Well, my Mum and some other people reckon that he would be really angry with me for not just getting on with life. But I don't think he would be at all. I think he would understand. I don't think he would be angry at all. [tearful]

What's it like for you when other people set themselves up as an authority on his voice? What is that like for you when other people say these things – that this is what Bill would have said, that he would have been angry with you for not doing ...?

It makes me feel sick inside.

It makes you feel sick inside ...

My sister's husband told me the day of the funeral just to: 'Get out there and be strong. Bill would have wanted you to be strong for him'. But I said, 'No, he would want me to be myself'.

This was your brother-in-law? Who said that Bill would just want you to be strong and go out there? And you said, 'No he wouldn't, he would want me to be myself'? What do you call that when other people somehow believe that they have the right to step into Bill's shoes? What's a good name for that?

I reckon that it's exceptionally egotistical on the behalf of that person doing it.

'Exceptionally egotistical' – that's a pretty kind description. It's a fairly kind description of something which seems, quite frankly, outrageous. But your sense is that Bill would say, 'No Sophia's doing the right thing for herself'? If he was here, is that what he would be saying?

[Sophia nods]

Do you have a sense of what else he would be saying if he was here? If I could just ask him right now, 'Bill, what is the most important thing about what Sophia has been saying?', what do you think he would be saying about that?

I think he would want me to do whatever it is I need to do for as long as I need to do it.

So, he would be saying, 'Sophia will do what she needs to do and that's right'. How would he respond to your resistance to all of these other people who pretend that they can speak with Bill's voice, or pretend that they know what is right for you? What would he say about your resistance to that? Would he be supportive of it, or would he ...

He would be very supportive.

How would he be supportive of it? What would he say?

He would tell me to listen to my own voice.

He would say listen to your own voice.

Yes.

What else would he say that would be supportive of your resistance? I'll just tell the group [turning to the reflecting team which is behind the one-way screen] that Bill wasn't a man of many words, was he? But what he had to say was very profound, wasn't it? When he spoke about things, he had a way of saying things that was very strong, quite economical ... but strong. Would you say that's true?

Yes.

So, what would be one of his economical and strong statements of support, for your resistance, that we might hear from Bill?

He would say that only I know what is right for me.

That's what he would say: 'Only Sophia knows what's right for her'.

[Sophia nods]

Is there anything else that occurs to you that he might say? Apart from: 'Listen to your own voice'. 'Only Sophia knows what's right for her'?

He always told me just to be me.

Just to be you? Okay ... I would like to ask a few more questions, but first I would like to know how this conversation is going for you. In the conversation that we are having here now, are we talking about the right things to be talking about?

Yes.

Why is that?

Because I have been beginning to doubt whether or not what I'm doing is right.

Because you've been beginning to doubt whether what you are doing is right. What's our conversation doing to that doubt?

It's reinforcing the belief to listen to myself, not to everyone else I know.

It's reinforcing your belief in listening to yourself, not to others?

I've spent too many years doing what other people thought I should be doing. It took me a long time to figure out what to do for myself. What felt right for me.

Can I write that down? Is that okay? You said, 'It took me a long time to figure out what to do for myself'. Is that what you said?

[Sophia nods]

Then you said something else.

I've spent such a long time doing everything that everyone else thought I should be doing.

What's it been like for you here to actually bring Bill into the room in the way that you have, just by sharing with me what his reactions would have been to our conversation? Is that something that has been a positive or negative experience for you? Or neither? To bring Bill's voice here.

I felt like he was here already anyway.

You felt he was here already?

When I was sitting downstairs.

When you were sitting downstairs, you felt he was here?

It just made me think about when we used to come here.

Is that a recent development for you, to actually experience him being with you in that way?

No. The other times when I've been here too, it's been the same.

It's when you come here that you've experienced that? You actually have a sense of his physical presence? What's that like to find him present physically like that when you come here?

It gives me moral support.

Gives you moral support? And you have that sense that he is right here with us now in a sense ... like ...

Yes. Where he always used to sit, next to me.

Sitting right next to you. Always on your left side?

On my right side.

On your right side ... sorry, I meant right side but I'm looking at you from here, on *my* left from where I'm sitting. On your right side. Has that happened anywhere else, Sophia, or is it just coming here that you experience his presence like this?

It's only here.

It's just here?

I think it's because Bill played such an important part here in helping me find me.

Yes, he did play a pretty powerful part didn't he? I'm just writing some things down, just in case I manage to get some of these down in a letter.

It's okay.

If you had this experience more, not just here at Dulwich Centre, but in other places too, would that be a positive or a negative thing? I was just thinking about what you know about your own healing.

It would be a positive thing.

'... it would be a positive thing'. [writing]

One of the things I find most scary is that he is not there to help me along the way any more.

But if he was there for you like he is here now, that would be a positive thing?

Yes.

How would that be helpful to you in terms of helping you along the way? If you could experience him in your life like you experience him here, in this room?

It's like whenever Bill was there for me even though he wasn't at the same place I was at ... not necessarily physically present ... but he was always there in my mind. There was a real safety in that.

Safety. So, he didn't have to be with you. He could be out and about. He didn't have to be there physically, but there was a place there that he occupied that contributed to safety for you?

It's a bit like having a guardian angel, I think.

A guardian angel! Do you think that this supports your understanding about what's healing for you – to have Bill in your life more, not to turn your back and get on with life?

I think it does, because otherwise I wouldn't feel his presence so easily.

You have actually ... brought forth Bill's presence for me more strongly just by what you've told me about feeling he was with you here and in the waiting room ... [tearful] And I can just see him. Didn't he used to slap his knee? Do you remember that? Wasn't that a common gesture – slapping his knee? What were some of his other common gestures? I remember that one so clearly. He would often just slap his knee ...

He would cross and uncross his legs.

That's right. Cross and uncross his legs, I remember that one too. And he would often be slightly outside of the situation, looking in on it, wouldn't he? He would be thinking all the time.

Lots of times I would be talking to him and I would think he wasn't quite listening, and I would say, 'Do you want me to continue saying what I'm talking about, or don't you really want to know?' He would say, 'I was listening all along'. I'd say, 'Well, what did I say?' So, then he would tell me. It was like he was always listening but thinking at the same time.

That brings back memories for me about talking to Bill here and thinking that he'd tuned out ...

But he didn't.

No. And I'd say, 'Bill, I don't know if you've been listening', and he would say, 'Well, I have been'. And I'd say, 'Well what did Sophia just say?' and he could give it back word for word.

[Sophia nods]

What's your guess about how I'm feeling?

I think you'd be feeling a sense of loss as well. At the same time, it's not like it's a total loss. [tearful]

You've hit the nail right on the head. I can speak about how it might not be a total loss, but you've helped me *experience* that it's not. Do you know what I mean? It's one thing to say it, but it's another thing to really experience it. What are you thinking about now?

Some of the time it just seems like it is a total loss for me.

Some of the time it does. Do you know … you've evoked his presence here very powerfully. I'm experiencing it as well, and I'm just wondering whether you know how you do that. Do you know? Because I know you said that it is partly coming here, but you go to other places that Bill was with you at. Do you know how you did that? You said that the first time that you came back here, a couple of months ago, you experienced his presence in the waiting-room. Do you know how you did that? Was it something you thought about before coming here, or was it something that just happened when you … ?

It just happened when I went in and sat down.

Do you know what sort of state of mind that you were in, that you got yourself into, that made that possible? Do you have any sense of that?

I just thought of Bill and when I thought of him it was like he was sitting there with me.

So, you thought about that in a way that didn't just evoke loss – it also evoked his presence as well?

I was just thinking about Bill, about his 'being', not just thinking about him as not being here physically any more.

121

So, you weren't thinking of that ... you were thinking of his being. That's what you were thinking about? If this could work for you in other places, if you could think of his being in the way that you did when you sat down in the waiting-room, would that be positive or negative or ... ?

I think it would be positive.

I can tell you that it's been positive for me. Even though it's been very emotional, it's been a positive experience for you to introduce his being here in the way that you have. I'm just wondering if we could figure out how you could take this sense of him being with you away from here and into other places, about how you might do that. Because it's not by chance it's happened here. I understand why you might do it here first, because of the part that Bill played in you having a life, having a voice. I'm just wondering what might make it possible for you to do this in other places. Do you have any thoughts about that? You said that you came here and you weren't thinking about ... what did you say you weren't thinking about?

I wasn't thinking about Bill in relation to loss necessarily. I was just thinking about him.

So, you were just thinking about his being ... his being.

I wasn't particularly thinking about him being dead.

I'd like to think of some questions that I could ask that would help me get more in touch with that skill of actually evoking Bill's presence in the way that you have – just to understand more about how you did that. I can understand that you came here and that you sat in the waiting-room and you just started thinking about his being, not his loss, and that's a part of it. Are you sensing his presence still with you right now?

He's here all the time in this room.

He's here all the time in this room. Okay. So, what he knew about you is present too. The really important understandings he had about you as a person, they're here as well?

[Sophia nods]

You've actually shared some of those understandings already, some of the understandings that he had of you. Some of the knowledges that he had about your life and about what works for you.

That's one of the scary things, because I don't know if I can do that.

You don't know if you can do it?

By myself, without having him …

Present. Yeah.

His support and encouragement and just … trying to understand. Not necessarily always understanding, but just accepting.

Accepting. And you were re-experiencing his acceptance here? His acceptance of you? His understanding of you? Accepting what he didn't understand, is that right?

[Sophia nods]

How does that affect you to experience that acceptance? Like right here. What is this doing to you to be experiencing this here?

It's like total affirmation of … just me.

Total affirmation of you?

Whatever was happening for me, whatever I was trying to struggle with, Bill just affirming that it was me and I could struggle with it. It wouldn't make me a bad person. Just me. Who I am today.

So that Bill could be with you in other places as well. And, there are some skills that you use in making him present, even for me – would it be okay if we talk about these skills? Are you interested in that?

[Sophia nods]

Why would you be interested in that?

It might help me in other places. And when I get into really black spaces it might be helpful to try and draw on that.

123

Yeah. That makes a lot of sense. Bill died about two months ago, is that correct?

Nine weeks today.

Nine weeks today, is it?

It's nine weeks since the last time that I saw him alive. He actually died on Wednesday morning.

Wednesday morning nine weeks ago. His acceptance of you didn't die and his understandings of you as a person have stayed with you because you've actually reintroduced them here today in this room.

Rupert

For a time our conversation took up further explorations of the knowledges and the skills that Sophia was expressing in bringing forth Bill's presence, and then she and I became an audience to the responses of the members of the reflecting team/outsider-witness group. Their rich re-tellings of the stories of Sophia and Bill's life were powerfully acknowledging of their relationship, and of the contributions that each had made to the other's life. These re-tellings also included accounts of how our conversation had powerfully touched the lives of some of the team members, and had presented them with options in the re-membering of lost loved ones in their own lives.

After the re-tellings of the reflecting team/outsider-witness group, and following Sophia's response to these re-tellings, I wondered aloud if she could identify anything in the room that she might take away with her and that could be a symbol of Bill's presence. I was thinking of Rupert. Rupert is one of my stuffed team members. He was gifted to me by Sophia over fifteen years ago, at a time when she was making her first tentative steps into life – Sophia is Rupert's creator. He is an extraordinary bear who had been making wonderful contributions to the lives of others for more than a decade and a half by teaming up with them in support of their desire to break free of the problems in their lives.

In response to my wondering, Sophia cast her eye around the room, and concluded, 'There is nothing here that could do this'. I asked if she would look again. In response, she asked, 'Is Rupert here?' He was. He had just returned to Dulwich Centre after being away with a family of a young child. On his return trip, he had suffered a misadventure. He had been riding in the family's car with his head out the window – something he loves to do – when he overbalanced and toppled out, to be run over by a bus. Fortunately Rupert is made of hardy stuff, and we soon managed to squeeze him back into shape, although we'd had to make an appointment at the Bear Clinic to have his ear repaired. He was still waiting on this appointment.

Sophia now had Rupert sitting on her lap. She was holding him affectionately.

Transcript (continued)

You were saying?

He [Bill] *was really rapt. I might take him and fix the ear* [referring to Rupert's injury].

You'll take him and fix the ear? You know that Rupert ...

We used to call him Stupid Rupert. [laughs]

'Stupid Rupert'! Did I tell you about what Rupert's done for a lot of the children that come along here? Are you aware of this? Do you know why he is so well worn?

Because he's been loved. [now smiling]

He's been loved. He goes home with some of the children who come here, and helps them out with their problems. And it is really interesting ... You were talking about Bill's acceptance, do you know what children experience with Rupert? Acceptance. No matter what they do, Rupert knows they're trying and he honours it.

I don't think he's stupid at all.

No, he's not is he. I think he's a comrade of Bill's. I think they're sort of comrades or something like that.

This is a kind of different teddy to the one I made and I always used to think that Rupert was a stupid-looking bear. That's why I called him Rupert the Stupid. [laughter]

He's turned out to be very smart. He doesn't tell me a whole lot about his wisdom – he keeps it to himself. He's a person of a few words, but these are pretty powerful words.

Like Bill!

Yes.

[Sophia is now tenderly stroking Rupert] *One of the things I've really missed is touching Bill.*

Do you think that taking Rupert away with you will play a part in contributing to you bringing Bill's presence forward in other places? ...

Postscript

Over the next couple of weeks Sophia had something of a breakthrough – she began to experience Bill's presence in her garden, particularly when she was tending his favourite shrubs. I wondered how it was that she had achieving this. Sophia's response: 'Anyone can do it. It is just natural. It is just a matter of clearing away the blocks and getting in touch with your strengths'. I asked Sophia how she would name these strengths, and wondered what else was at play here: 'Others can also name similar strengths. Yet, despite identifying these strengths in this way, experiencing the presence of the voices of their lost loved ones remains an elusive achievement. Could I ask some questions about what it is that you are bringing to these strengths?' Sophia was interested, and so a conversation was begun that was identifying of some of the skills and knowledges that she was expressing in bringing forth Bill's presence.

It was in this conversation that Sophia for the first time became conscious of the fact that she had kept a place in her life for her father's voice since his death, when she was a young girl, twenty-eight years ago.

As she spoke of this realisation, and of her father's life, she related stories of his sisters, her aunts, who had remained in Holland and whom she had never met, but whose images had been sustaining of her in the many difficult times in her life. 'How is it that you knew them so well when you had never met them? How do you understand this?' I asked. Sophia spoke of her father's stories of life in Holland, and of the central part that his sisters played in these stories. We talked for a while about what it was about her father's story-telling that had so powerfully evoked the images of her aunts. Sophia then concluded that her father must have had the knowledges and the skills that made it possible for him to experience the ongoing presence of the voices of his sisters when so far away from them and from his birthplace in Holland, and that this must have been very sustaining of him in his life in Australia. Sophia also concluded that her father had passed these knowledges and skills on to her, and that it was through these that she had been able keep a place for his and for her aunts' voices in her life, despite all that she had been through. Further, in this conversation, Sophia stepped more fully into the realisation that she had been putting these knowledges and skills to work in my room and in her garden in her desire to have Bill rejoin her life.

In reflecting on our conversation, I asked Sophia: 'If you have put these knowledges and skills to work in keeping a place in your life for your father for twenty-eight years, do you think they might do the same for you in maintaining your connection with Bill? And if so, at what age will you be before you need to worry about whether or not there is some risk that you could leave Bill behind?' Sophia believed these knowledges and skills would continue to be available to her, and figured that she need not worry about the risk of leaving Bill behind until she was seventy-two years of age. This was a startling realisation, and with this she felt significant relief. What Sophia had feared most was that her life might go forward and that Bill might be left behind.

As our conversation turned to Rupert's contribution, I became aware of the fact that Sophia was already passing these skills onto her grand-daughter, Latoya. Latoya had become very attached to Rupert, and whenever these two were together, she would speak to Sophia of her 'Poppy'. Over the next few months the experience of Bill's presence became increasingly available to Sophia. He was re-membered into her life.

Notes

1. At times it has been assumed that this work that is oriented to the 'saying hullo again' metaphor is also informed by a notion of a spirituality that is immanent or ascendant, and that is associated with forces that are other-worldly, or of another plane or dimension. These notions are not ones that have shaped the development of this work, and this is not what I have intended to propose. Rather, work that is oriented by the 'saying hullo again' metaphor assists persons in the development of skills in the resurrection and expression of significant experiences of their relationships. These are experiences that these persons have lived through – that are part of their stock of lived-experience.

2. There was a reflecting team/outsider-witness group present for the interview that this transcript was drawn from. Because Sophia spoke very quietly, I reflected back most of what she said so that the members of this reflecting team might hear our conversation.

References

Myerhoff, B. (1982). Life history among the elderly: Performance, visibility, and re-membering. In J. Ruby (Ed.), *A crack in the mirror: Reflective perspectives in anthropology* (pp. 99–117). Philadelphia, PA: University of Pennsylvania Press.

White, M. (1988). Saying hullo again: The incorporation of the lost relationship in the resolution of grief. *Dulwich Centre Newsletter*, (Spring), 7–11.

chapter five

Children, trauma and subordinate storyline development
by Michael White

Children are not strangers to trauma. In most societies around the globe the incidence of the abuse of children remains high despite many initiatives undertaken by state and community organisations to address this. And in most parts of the world that are experiencing the calamities associated with war, disease, displacement, and economic turmoil, children remain most acutely vulnerable to life-threatening hardship and trauma. Service providers who work in local child-protection services with the families of refugees, and those who work with people in parts of the world that are ravaged by war and disease, will be acutely aware of the importance of assisting children to recover from the effects of the trauma they have been subject to. And they will also be aware of the importance of doing this in ways that are psychologically and emotionally safe for these children who have experienced so little physical safety in the history of their young lives and, in many circumstances, when the achievement of this physical safety cannot be guaranteed.

The importance of attending to this safety is underscored by the reluctance of many children, who have been through trauma, to speak of their experience of this trauma. While there are numerous theories about this reluctance – for example, that this is due to psychological mechanisms of denial and suppression – it would seem that concerns about retribution should the trauma of abuse be disclosed, and about the potential risk of reliving trauma in the context of giving voice to this, are high on the list of relevant understandings of children's reluctance to speak of their experiences of trauma. This concern about encountering re-traumatisation upon giving expression to experiences of trauma will be a significant focus of the discussion in this paper.

I believe this concern is well-founded, for there is an ever-potential hazard that, in speaking of their experiences of trauma, children will be re-traumatised; that children will become trapped in the immediacy of their experience of the trauma they have lived through; that they will be ensnared in the reliving of this experience. This very outcome can be witnessed in circumstances in which children give voice to their experience of trauma in ways that contribute to a reinforcement of the negative conclusions they hold about their identity and about their lives. This, in turn, is usually associated with an escalation of a sense of shame, of vulnerability, of hopelessness, of desolation, and of futility. If great care is not taken in building a context in which what might be called 'psychological and emotional safety' is ascertained for the child, then there is a strong chance that the child, in response to encouragement to express their experience of trauma, will find themselves redefined by the trauma they have been subject to.

This assertion is not founded upon 'armchair' observation. Over the years I have met with many children in many contexts who have been re-traumatised through the very efforts that have been undertaken to assist them to address experiences of trauma. And on occasions I have had the excruciating experience of witnessing such re-traumatisation in process when I have not been in a position to influence the shape of the 'healing practices' being administered.

Repositioning

Attention to this aspect of psychological and emotional safety in working with children who have been subject to trauma cannot be too strongly emphasised. How can we ensure that children are not vulnerable to an experience of re-traumatisation in the context of speaking about what they have been through? This question encourages considerations of the 'psychological positioning' of the child in opening space for them to address their experiences of trauma. Another way of stating this:

this question leads us to considerations of the territory of identity that the child is standing in as they go about putting expression to their experiences of abuse. If this is a territory of identity that is circumscribed by the trauma that the child has been subject to, then it can be predicted that to simply encourage the child to give expression to their experiences of this trauma will be re-traumatising, and that this will contribute to a renewed sense of vulnerability.

In addressing options for the sort of re-positioning of children that will provide a safe context for them to give expression to their experiences of trauma, narrative practices that enable the identification and rich development of the subordinate storylines of these children's lives can be employed. As these subordinate storylines are developed, they provide an alternative territory of identity for children to take recourse to in speaking of their experiences of trauma. In this chapter I will focus on options for the development of these subordinate storylines and on how these can establish territories of safety for children who have been subject to trauma.

In emphasising this focus, I don't want to be misunderstood on the subject of supporting children to speak about their experiences of trauma. It is clearly important for children to have the opportunity to speak of trauma and its consequences; to be provided with support in putting to words that which has not been spoken. I have consistently found that when children have territories of identity available to them which provide the sort of safety I have been describing, they invariably engage in powerful expressions of their experiences of trauma and its consequences. And these are expressions of the sort that provide an antidote to the sense of shame, hopelessness, desolation, and futility that is invariably reinforced in the context of retraumatisation.

Subordinate storyline development

The genesis of subordinate storyline development[1] is to be found in children's responses to the trauma they have been subject to. No child is a passive recipient of trauma, regardless of the nature of this trauma. Amongst other things, children take action to minimise their exposure to trauma and to decrease their vulnerability to it by modifying the traumatic episodes they are subject to, or by finding ways of modifying the effects of this trauma on their lives. However, it is rare for children's responses to the traumas of their lives to be acknowledged. It is more common for these responses to go unnoticed, or to be punished, or to be disqualified through ridicule and diminishment within the trauma context.

These responses to trauma and its consequences are founded upon what children give value to, upon what they hold precious in their lives. And these responses reflect knowledges about, and skills in:

a. the preservation of life in life-threatening contexts,

b. finding support in hostile environments,

c. establishing domains of safety in unsafe places,

d. holding onto possibilities for life in circumstances that are discouraging of this,

e. developing nurturing responses to others in situations that are degrading of such responses,

f. finding connection and a sense of affiliation with others in settings that are isolating,

g. refusing to visit trauma on the lives of others in milieus that are encouraging of this reproduction of trauma,

h. healing from the consequences of trauma under conditions that are unfavourable to this,

i. achieving degrees of self-acceptance in atmospheres that are sponsoring of self-rejection,

j. and more.

These knowledges and skills are rarely independently constructed and developed by children who have been subject to trauma. Rather, it is invariably the case that these knowledges and skills have been constructed and developed in partnership with other children and with adults who are also subject to, or who have been subject to, trauma. And, further, this collaboration in the construction and development of these knowledges and skills is usually very significantly shaped by specific familial, community and cultural ethos.

In addressing this subject of children's responses to trauma, and in naming some of the knowledges and skills expressed in these responses, I am not suggesting that trauma is anything but painful for children, that it does not have highly negative consequences for the lives of children who are subject to it, or that this experience of trauma and its consequences does not need to be addressed. And I am not suggesting that for children to hold onto what they give value to, or to develop knowledges and skills of the sort to which I have referred, is enough to mitigate this pain and these consequences. My intention in drawing attention to the significance of these responses to trauma is to emphasise the fact that the negative consequences of trauma do not represent the whole story of a child's life and identity, and to give an account of some of the 'material' that is ever-available for the sort of subordinate storyline development that constructs alternative territories of identity that can be occupied by children in giving expression to their experience of trauma. These are alternative territories of identity that will make it possible for children to give expression to their experiences of trauma but not be re-traumatised in the process of doing so.

In regard to this appreciation of the fact that the negative consequences of trauma do not represent the whole story of children's lives, it can be helpful to think of memories of trauma that exclude an account of children's responses to trauma as 'half memories'. In the context of this understanding, subordinate storyline development contributes to 'full memory' restoration. I believe this 'full memory' restoration to be critically important in therapeutic consultations with children who have been subject to trauma.

Subordinate storyline development in work with children who have been subject to trauma contributes to the rich description of the child's responses to trauma, and of what these responses reflect in terms of:

1. What children give value to; of what they hold precious – which includes specific beliefs, guiding principles, hopes, dreams, personal integrities, personal ethics, and so on.

2.   What children intend for their lives – which includes specific purposes, goals, ambitions, objectives, wishes, quests, pursuits, aspirations, and so on.

3.   The knowledges and skills expressed in these responses – which includes the knowledges and skills associated with the points on page 132: a. through to j.

4.   The social, relational and cultural genesis of these responses – which includes the contribution of significant figures in the child's history (including peers), specific family legacies that can be honoured, significant children's literature, edifying cultural myth, ethnic traditions and concepts of spirituality, and so on.

In regard to this fourth point, as previously stated, the knowledges and skills expressed in children's responses to trauma are rarely independently constructed and developed by these children, but are developed in partnership with others, as is what children hold precious and what they intend for their lives. When the social, relational and cultural genesis of these knowledges and skills, and of what children hold precious, and of what they intend for their lives, is revealed in the context of subordinate story-line development, there are opportunities for children to experience the stories of their lives linked anew with the stories of the lives of others. Many of these others are significant figures in the child's history, and as the contribution of these figures becomes more visible, new opportunities are presented for these children to connect/ reconnect with their relational/social/community networks. This can be in part facilitated by supporting children in the identification of, and in the explicit acknowledgement of, the contribution of these figures. Such acknowledgement can take many forms, including in the form of letters and certificates of recognition co-developed/co-written by children and their counsellors/community workers, and in the form of honouring ceremonies for these figures planned by children in collaboration with these counsellors/community workers.

The accounts of what children hold precious, and of what they intend for their lives that are featured in subordinate storyline development can be thought of as concepts about life and about identity. The extent to which children have formed these concepts is dependent upon the stage and state of the child's development, and even for older children these concepts are rarely fully formed. In consultations that contribute to subordinate storyline development for children, these concepts are not usually 'discovered' completely formed, but are further developed in the context of therapeutic conversations in which the counsellor/community worker is a conversational partner. It is my understanding that such conceptual development is critical to the establishment of children's ability to intervene in shaping their own lives and of their ability to influence their relationships with others (Vygotsky, 1986).

I have reiterated the point that, in rendering more visible the sources of children's responses to trauma, subordinate storyline development provides a safe place for children to stand in the context of giving voice to the trauma they have been subject to, and to the consequences of this trauma. But this is not all. This subordinate storyline development also provides a foundation for action for children to proceed with their lives. As these subordinate storylines become more richly known and experienced, it becomes more possible for children to take initiatives that are in harmony with what they give value to, with what they intend for their lives, and that are shaped by the knowleges and skills that are of their own histories. It also becomes more possible for them to further develop their connections with those who are significant to them, and with valued aspects of culture and history.

In focussing on the subject of subordinate storyline development in this paper, there is a risk that I will be understood to be suggesting that the conversations of narrative therapy are revealing of an alternative story that is the 'true' or 'authentic' story. However, this is not the case. To the contrary, I understand life to be multi-storied, and all of the alternative stories of life to be cultural, relational and historical in origin; these stories are all possible constructions of the events and experiences of life. And in subordinate storyline development, I am aware that there are often opportunities for people to experience being positioned simultaneously in more than one field of existence, in more than one territory of identity.

Personal agency

In rendering more visible children's responses to trauma according to the terms that I have defined here, subordinate storyline development restores children's sense of personal agency. This is a sense of self that is associated with the perception that one is able to have some effect on the shape of one's own life – a sense that one is able to intervene in one's own life as an agent of what one gives value to and as an agent of one's own intentions, and a sense that the world is at least minimally responsive to the fact of one's existence.

The restoration and/or development of this sense of personal agency in work with children who have been subject to trauma is of critical importance. The restoration and/or development of this sense of personal agency provides an antidote to the sort of highly disabling conclusions about one's identity that feature perceptions that one is a passive recipient of life's forces. Such perceptions are highly influential in the development of conclusions that one is 'damaged' and 'messed up' on account of what one has been through, and to the development of the pervasive and profoundly immobilising phenomena of 'vulnerability' and 'fragility'.

The contribution that subordinate storyline development might make as an antidote to these negative identity conclusions that children have often derived is of critical importance, particularly in these contemporary times in which the discourses of victimhood have become so influential in the construction of the identities of people who have been subject to trauma. These discourses have become prominent in the professional and the popular psychologies, and not only promote the construction of disabled identities, but also shape relationship practices that are diminishing and marginalising of people who have been through significant trauma. In the context of these relationship practices, people who have been subject to significant trauma become the 'other'. It is in the context of these relationship practices that their identity is constructed as 'spoiled'.

In regard to service provision, when workers are encouraged to place their sole focus on the trauma that children have been subject to, and on the consequences of this trauma, they become vulnerable to the reproduction of these discourses of victimhood in their therapeutic work. In this circumstance, there is a risk that counsellors/community workers will further diminish children's sense of personal agency and, as well, inadvertently reinforce a passive-recipient identity status for these children. This central and exclusive focus on trauma and its consequences obscures the extent to which identity is constructed in language and in the context of relational practices. And it obscures the extent to which it is identity that is very much at stake in work with children who have been subject to abuse.

This is an important matter, for the contemporary discourses of victimhood have serious consequences for child development, and can contribute very significantly to the long-term establishment of a sense of 'emptiness' and 'desolation' in life. These contemporary discourses of victimhood also have serious consequences for the therapeutic relationship in work with children. Although many therapists/community workers have an awareness of the conditions that can contribute to the development of 'learned helplessness' in the people who seek their help, this term is far too mild a description of the potential devastation that these discourses of victimhood can wreak in young people's lives.

I believe that the modern and popular interpretation of the concept of catharsis has played a significant role in obscuring the play of these discourses of victimhood. This interpretation of this concept is associated with the idea that human action is founded upon an emotional/psychological system that works according to the principles of hydraulic and steam-engine technology – for example, that emotions are held under pressure within this system like a head of steam is held under pressure in a steam engine, and that the 'discharge' or 'release' of this pressure through the appropriate 'valve' will culminate in the desired outcome. According to this concept, the pain of trauma is held under pressure in the emotional/psychological system, and the discharge of this pain via an appropriate avenue will be a panacea in regard to the effects of this trauma. Under the sway of this interpretation of the concept of catharsis, counsellors often encourage people to give expression to their experiences of trauma without engaging with considerations about the safety of doing so; without a foundation for contemplating the potential for this to be re-traumatising for people, for understanding how this might be constructing of people's identity, and without a foundation for grasping the critical importance of the resurrection and/or development of a sense of personal agency for the people who are consulting them.

Identification of children's responses to trauma

I have referred to the part that the rich description of children's responses to trauma can play in subordinate storyline development, with specific reference to:

a.   what children give value to,

b.   what children intend for their lives,

c.   the knowledges and skills expressed in these responses, and to

d.   the social, relational and cultural genesis of these responses.

This begs the question: 'How can these responses be identified?' There are many avenues of therapeutic inquiry that render visible and richly describe children's responses to trauma. I will now draw out three of these avenues of therapeutic inquiry:

•   identifying the absent but implicit,

•   reflecting on problem-solving activity, and

•   direct observation of spontaneous interaction.

I will also provide descriptions of therapeutic consultations with children which are based on each of these avenues of inquiry.

Identifying the absent but implicit

The notion of the 'absent but implicit' is associated with the idea that, in order to express one's experiences of life, one must distinguish this experience from what it is not. By this account, every expression can be considered to be founded upon its contrast, which I refer to as the 'absent but implicit'. I have drawn significantly from the work of Jaques Derrida (1973, 1976, 1978) in this understanding, which I have discussed at some length elsewhere (White, 2000, 2003). For many years I have found this notion to be of service in the genesis of the subordinate storylines of people's lives. Amongst other possibilities, the notion of the absent but implicit provides opportunities for ongoing psychological pain in response to trauma to be considered a testimony to the significance of what it was that the person held precious that was violated through the experience of trauma. (See box: 'The absent but implicit'.)

The absent but implicit

To clarify the implications of this understanding, I will here reproduce part of a discussion from 'Narrative practice and community assignments' (White, 2003, pp. 39–43). This discussion presents alternative perspectives on psychological pain and emotional distress that are derived from the notion of the 'absent but implicit'.

Pain as testimony

Ongoing psychological pain in response to trauma in the history of people's lives might be considered a testimony to the significance of what it was that the person held precious that was violated through the experience of trauma. This can include people's understandings about:

a. cherished purposes for one's life;
b. prized values and beliefs around acceptance, justice and fairness;
c. treasured aspirations, hopes and dreams;
d. moral visions about how things might be in the world;
e. significant pledges, vows and commitments about ways of being in life; etc.

If psychological pain can be considered to be a testimony to such purposes, values, beliefs, aspirations, hopes, dreams, moral visions, and commitments, then the experienced intensity of this pain can be considered to be a reflection of the degree to which these intentional states were held precious by persons. In the context of therapeutic conversations, these intentional state understandings can be identified, resurrected and become richly known. As well, it is within these conversations that people have the opportunity to experience being at one with a range of positive identity conclusions that displace many negative 'truths' of identity that they have been recruited into as an outcome of the traumas they have been subject to.

Distress as tribute

Day-to-day emotional distress in response to trauma in people's histories might be considered a tribute to their ability to maintain a constant relationship with all of those purposes, values, beliefs, aspirations, hopes, dreams, visions and commitments held precious – to their refusal to relinquish or to be separated from what that was so powerfully disrespected and demeaned in the context of trauma, from what it was that they continue to revere.

If such emotional distress can be considered to be a tribute to people's determination to maintain a constant relationship with that which was powerfully disrespected and demeaned in the context of trauma, then the experienced intensity of this distress can be considered to be a reflection of the degree to which the person has continued to revere and maintain a relationship with what it is that they hold precious. In the context of therapeutic conversations, acknowledgement of people's refusal to relinquish what was so powerfully disrespected, and explorations of their skills in maintaining a relationship with these intentional states, can be very significantly elevating of their sense of who they are, and of what their lives are about.

Pain and distress as proclamation of response

If ongoing psychological pain can be considered a testimony to the significance of what it was that the person held precious that was violated through the experience of trauma, and if emotional distress can be considered a tribute to their ability to maintain a constant relationship with what was so powerfully disrespected and demeaned in the context of trauma, exploring the specifics of this testimony and tribute can provide a basis for identifying people's responses to the trauma they have been subject to. People respond to the crises of their lives, even when these crises are the outcome of trauma under circumstances in which they are relatively powerless to escape the context or to bring about a cessation of whatever it is that they are being subject to. Even small children who are being subject to abuse respond in ways to modify what it is that they are being subject to. These acts of redress that are shaped by people's intentional states are rarely recognised and acknowledged, and therefore rarely appreciated by and held with reverence by the people who initiate them.

When the specifics of what psychological pain and emotional distress might be a testimony or tribute to are defined, this can provide a basis for explorations of the extent to which this pain and distress is also a proclamation of people's responses to the traumas that they have been subject to. In the context of therapeutic conversations, what it is that a person held precious and has continued to revere can become known, and this provides the basis for an inquiry into how this shaped their responses to what they were being put through. This sort of inquiry is one that emphasises actions taken that reflect the exercise of personal agency according to specific intentional states.

Psychological pain and distress as elements of a legacy
Psychological pain and emotional distress might be understood to be elements of a legacy expressed by people who, in the face of the non-responsiveness of the world around them, remain resolute in their determination that the trauma that they and others have gone through will not be for nothing – that things must change on account of what they have gone through. According to this understanding, despite the absence of a wider acknowledgement that things must change, these people are sentinels who will not let this matter drop, and who have remained on guard against

forces that would be diminishing of their experiences, and that would be reproducing of trauma in the lives of others.

This understanding contributes to a context in which the legacy that is represented in expressions of psychological pain and emotional distress can be significantly honoured and joined with by others. It can also contribute to a context that is acknowledging of the way in which people rely upon their insider experience of trauma in recognising the consequences of this in the lives of others, and in responding to others with a compassion that touches their lives, and that evokes a sense of solidarity with them.

Deanne

Deanne, ten years of age, had been referred to me with an explicit request that I assist her to express her experiences of very significant trauma that she'd been subject to. Various efforts to achieve this had already been undertaken in three different counselling contexts, but the outcome of these efforts had been largely negative. In response to these efforts, Deanne had become highly distressed, then regressed and, following each instance, had felt quite unstable for a period of weeks.

At the outset of my meetings with Deanne I made it clear that I had no expectations in regard to her speaking about the trauma that she'd been put through, but enquired as to whether it would be okay to ask her a few questions about the distress that she'd been managing. This was okay by Deanne, so I initiated an inquiry into what it might be that was precious to her that had been hurt by the abuse she'd experienced, suggesting that the intensity of this distress might correspond with the strength to which she held whatever it was precious in her life; with perhaps the degree of passion that she felt for what she gave value to in her life. In response to these questions, Deanne began to talk about her sense of the unfairness of what she'd been through, and this led to a conversation about specific principles of fairness that had always been important to her. Before long I was hearing stories about some of the initiatives of Deanne's life that were a reflection of these principles, including one about action that she'd recently been taking in solidarity with another girl at school who'd also been through hard times and who was the subject of peer abuse.

In our second meeting, amongst other things, we embarked upon explorations of the history of these principles of fairness in Deanne's life. It was in these explorations that Deanne for the first time established a link between her voice on these principles of fairness, and one of her favourite books – *Pippi Longstocking* (Lindgren, 1950). In our third meeting, we did some shared reading of the passages of *Pippi Longstocking* that Deanne was most drawn to, and in which these principles were expressed. This meeting culminated with me assisting Deanne to write a letter to Astrid Lindgren, Pippi Longstocking's creator, which acknowledged this author's contribution to Deanne's sense of fairness. Deanne clearly experienced joy in this task.

For our fourth meeting, with Deanne's approval, I invited some other young people to join as outsider-witnesses.[2] These were young people who'd consulted me about trauma in the past, and who'd volunteered to join me in my work with other young people who might be following in their footsteps. The powerfully resonant re-tellings of Deanne's story by these outsider witnesses had a very positive effect on Deanne's conclusions about her own identity.

In our fifth meeting, at which these outsider witnesses were again present, I found opportunity to consult Deanne about her thoughts on whether her principles of fairness had played a role in her survival of the trauma that she'd been through. Her response was in the affirmative, and led to a conversation about the ways in which these principles had shaped her responses to this trauma. As these responses were drawn out Deanne began to speak openly of the specific details of this trauma and, although this was an emotional time for her, there was not a hint that she was encountering any retraumatisation or regression as an outcome of this. Again, the re-tellings of the outsider witnesses were powerfully resonant for Deanne – this time the focus of these re-tellings was placed on Deanne's experience of trauma, its consequences, and on her response to this.

At our sixth meeting, I learned that Deanne had not experienced any destabilising effects from giving such direct expression to her experience of abuse. Rather, she experienced her life proceeding in unexpectedly positive ways. This emboldened her to put more words to what she'd previously been unable to speak of and, as one outcome of so doing, Deanne found that this didn't upset her in the way that she'd predicted it would. To Deanne, this was, of itself, a valued learning, and a significantly positive reflection on her personal development.

Upon reviewing, with Deanne, the contribution of the re-tellings of outsider witnesses, it became quite clear that these had played a highly significant role in the acknowledgement of the trauma, its consequences, and of Deanne's response to this trauma. It also became quite clear that these re-tellings played a significant role in the restoration of and further development of her sense of personal agency.

Reflecting on problem-solving activity

Problem-solving activity can provide a fertile context for rendering visible what it is that children give value to, what they intend for their lives, and the knowledges of life and skills of living that are important to them. In witnessing children engaging in such activity, counsellors/ community workers can note children's responses to the task to be solved and their responses to each other as they go about addressing the task. Following this, these children can be interviewed about these responses, and about their further reflections on the experience of the problem-solving activity.

Imbrahim, Amir, and Alex

I was meeting with Imbrahim, Amir, and Alex, who had migrated from their countries of origin as refugees. They had been referred to me on account of concerns about their generally withdrawn status, and about the extent to which they had continued to maintain silence in regard to the very significant trauma that they had been subject to over an extended period ahead of their migration.

We'd taken a walk together in a nearby park. On account of a recent storm, the small creek in this park had been turned into a torrent. The three boys determined that this would have to be traversed, and set about figuring out how this might be done – the creek was not deep and could not have swept them away, but there was a very real risk that they could have fallen in and become wet through. With the aid of various props that they found in the park, in a spirit of challenge and adventure, and with each other's support, eventually all three had succeeded in crossing to and fro without getting wet.

Afterwards we sat and talked about what had gone into the task that had ensured its success. Imbrahim, Amir and Alex's reflections on this, along with their verbal utterances that had accompanied the adventure itself, provided me with a foundation to interview them about what they held precious, and about their intentional understandings of their actions. I will include here a small sample of the sort of questions that shaped this interview:

Questions of Imbrahim

Imbrahim, you said that at one point you'd been scared for Alex, more scared for him than you'd been for yourself. And you also said that this was about 'looking out for others'.

- *What did this 'looking out for others' make possible for you in the creek adventure?*
- *What is your guess about what this did for Amir and Alex?*
- *How did you feel about making this contribution?*
- *What does this say about what is important to you?*
- *Can you tell me some other stories of your life that reflect this ability to 'look out for others'?*

Questions of Amir

Amir, I heard you say something about how at one point you worried that it couldn't be done, but that you kept on because you knew how good it would feel when you did get to the other side.

- *What is a good name for how you keep trying to get to the other side when things are difficult or scary?*

- *How did this play a part in the creek adventure working out like it did?*
- *How did you feel about playing this part?*
- *I understand that it was about 'keeping on trying' and 'knowing that things will be better' when you get to the other side. Would you say something about what you have learned in your life about getting through things that are difficult?*
- *Can you tell me some stories about your life that reflect these learnings about getting through things that are difficult?*

Questions of Alex

Alex, you said that you set a goal for yourself, and that you were not going to give up on this goal, no matter what. What is a good name for this capacity to hold onto goals that are important to you, and to see these through?

- *How did this affect what you did in the creek adventure?*
- *What was it like for you to find yourself holding onto this goal in the way that you did?*
- *What does this say about what you want for your life?*
- *Can you tell me some stories about your life that are examples of you refusing to let go of your goals, and that are examples of standing for what you want in life?*

I had several more meetings with Imbrahim, Amir, and Alex, and these provided the opportunity for me to enquire into the relational/social/cultural histories of what these young men held precious, of their intentional understandings of their actions, and of the knowledges and skills that were richly described in our conversations. One outcome of the conversations that were generated by this line of enquiry was that Imbrahim, Amir, and Alex realised that the stories of their lives were linked to valued stories of their cultural history in ways that they could rejoice in.

When I sensed that subordinate storyline development was such that it afforded alternative and relatively secure territories of identity for these young men to occupy, I began to consult them about whether what they held precious and what they intended for their lives, along with these various capacities, knowledges and skills, had played part in them getting through the trauma they'd experienced. The response was a unanimous 'yes'. In the context of providing an account of this, these three young men gave vivid detail to their experiences of trauma. I encouraged them to reflect on what it was like for them to be giving voice to the hard things they'd been through, and learned that this was the first time that they'd been able to speak of this without feeling 'absolutely terrible' afterward.

My latter meetings with Imbrahim, Amir, and Alex were structured around outsider-witness practices. In these meetings they took turns for each other in the development of re-tellings of the trauma they'd each been through, of the consequences of this, and of their responses to this trauma. These re-tellings were highly significant in the acknowledgement of the trauma and its consequences, and of their responses to this trauma. And, as with Deanne, for each boy these re-tellings played a significant role in the restoration and further development of their sense of personal agency.

Direct observation of spontaneous interaction

Direct observation of the spontaneous interaction of children who have been subject to trauma can provide clues about points of entry for subordinate storyline development.

James, Emily and Beth

In my first meeting with James (11 years), Emily (8 years), and Beth (7 years), siblings who had been through very significant abuse and neglect in their young lives, on several occasions I witnessed James engaging in the care-taking of his sisters. This care-taking was evident in several ways, including in the patience that he expressed in assisting Emily and Beth to clarify what they thought about some relatively simple subjects that I consulted them about.

This observation provided a foundation for a therapeutic inquiry in which, amongst other things, I encouraged James, Emily and Beth to:

a.   name these care-taking skills,

b.   describe the know-how that was expressed in these skills,

c.   define the contribution of these skills to Emily's life and Beth's life,

d.   speculate about what the possession of these skills might make possible for James in the future of his own life,

e.   reflect on what these skills might say about what is most important to James,

f.   trace the history of the development of these skills in James' life, and to

g.   identify figures of James' history who might have valued and appreciated these skills, and who might be implicated in his development of these skills.

As it turned out that James' teacher from his third grade was a figure who was implicated in the development of his care-taking skills, she was invited to our third, fourth, and fifth meetings. In the role of outsider witness, this teacher played a very significant part in the rich development of a subordinate storyline of James' life, in the acknowledgement of the trauma that James (as well as Emily and Beth) had been subject to, and in the restoration and further development of his sense of personal agency.

Emily's and Beth's responsiveness to James' care-taking did not go unnoticed. This provided the foundation for explorations that were focussed on how they had been able to open themselves to the concern and support of others, and on their skills in connecting with others.

When the time seemed right, I began to enquire about whether these skills had had a part to play in providing a foundation for these children to get through the hard times they'd experienced. At this point, all three children became quite animated in giving accounts of how they had used these skills to survive the abuse and neglect that had been visited upon them. These were dramatic and vivid accounts, which included specific details of what they had been subject to, which they had mostly never previously spoken of. Over several more meetings it was clear that James, Emily and Beth now had a foundation for giving voice to their experiences of abuse and neglect in ways that were not accompanied by a risk that they would be defined by this abuse and neglect, in ways that were not accompanied by a risk that they could be re-traumatised in this.

Conclusion

In this paper, I have emphasised the importance of subordinate storyline development in consultations with children who have been subject to trauma. This subordinate storyline development provides an alternative territory of identity for children to stand in as they begin to give voice to their experiences of trauma. This affords children a significant degree of immunity from the potential for re-traumatisation in response to therapeutic initiatives to assist them to speak of their experiences of trauma and its consequences. I have also provided some illustrations of the implications of these ideas for consultations with children who have been subject to trauma. In a future paper on this subject I intend to illustrate the relevance of these considerations to younger children.

In emphasising these considerations of safety, it is not my intention to sponsor avoidance, on behalf of counsellors and community workers, of the facts of the trauma that children have been subject to. And in my own work with people who have been subject to trauma, I have not sought to attenuate their expressions of trauma and its consequences. I have not been timid in opening space for people to speak of what they have not had the opportunity to speak of, to put words to what has been unmentionable. This has been so for my meetings with people who have been subject to a range of abuses, including political torture, and for people struggling with trauma that is the outcome of a range of social calamities, including disease epidemics. However, I have taken care to do what is within my understandings and skills to establish contexts in which people can give full voice to their experiences of trauma in ways that enable them to wrest their lives from the prospective longer term consequences of this trauma. And I have never accepted that any person need be re-traumatised in the context of assisting them to address what they have been through.

Notes

1. I will refer to 'subordinate storyline' development when describing the further development of some of the alternative stories of children's lives that are to be found in thin traces, in the shadows of the dominant stories of their lives. This description seems apt, as it is not by chance that these storylines are relatively invisible at the outset of therapeutic conversations. These storylines have been subordinated in the context of the politics of disqualification, diminishment, ridicule and marginalisation.

2. Outsider-witness participation is a regular feature of my consultations. For an account of the scaffolding of outsider-witness participation in therapeutic practice, and of the tradition of acknowledgement that shapes the re-tellings of outsider witnesses, see White 2004a & 2004b.

References

Derrida, J. (1973). *Speech and phenomena, and other essays on Husserl's Theory of Signs.* Evanston, IL: Northwestern University Press.

Derrida, J. (1976). *Of grammatology.* Baltimore, MD: John Hopkins University Press.

Derrida, J. (1978). *Writing and difference.* London, UK: Routledge and Kegan Paul.

Lindgren, A. (1950). *Pippi Longstocking.* New York, NY: Viking Press

Vygotsky, L. (1986). *Thought and language.* Cambridge, MA: The MIT Press.

White, M. (2000). Re-engaging with history: The absent but implicit. In M. White, *Reflections on narrative practice: Essays and interviews* (pp. 35–58). Adelaide, Australia: Dulwich Centre Publications.

White, M. (2003). Narrative practice and community assignments. *The International Journal of Narrative Therapy and Community Work,* (2), 17–55.

White, M. (2004a). Narrative practice, couple therapy and conflict dissolution. In M. White, *Narrative practice and exotic lives: Resurrecting diversity in everyday life* (pp. 1–41). Adelaide, Australia: Dulwich Centre Publications.

White, M. (2004b). Working with people who are suffering the consequences of multiple trauma: A narrative perspective. *The International Journal of Narrative Therapy and Community Work,* (1), 47–76.

chapter six

Narrative practice and the unpacking of identity conclusions
by Michael White

Daniel[1]

Daniel, a sad looking boy of eleven years of age, was brought to see me by his parents, Tom and Lucy, who were at their wits' end. They complained that their lives were being destroyed by Daniel. According to them, he was 'bringing trouble down' on their lives in every way imaginable. He had been expelled from two schools, and was now suspended from a third. He was in trouble with the police, with neighbours, with the parents of his peers, and, as well, was creating havoc at home. As I listened to these details, it was clear to me that Lucy and Tom were attributing very sinister motives to Daniel's actions. In fact their account of these events was laced with a range of highly negative conclusions about Daniel's identity, and these were painful for me to hear. Amongst other things, they had concluded that 'he was out to destroy the family', that he was a 'worthless good-for-nothing', 'useless to himself and everyone else', and a 'dead loss when it came to efforts to do anything for him'. Daniel's response to all of this seemed one of studied indifference. He just sat there, neither confirming nor protesting this account of his life and identity. But I had the sense that he felt himself to be at one with these very negative conclusions.

I said that on hearing these details I was developing some appreciation of just how frustrating the situation must be. Tom responded to this, exclaiming: 'And you don't even know the half of it yet!' My response: 'Would it be okay then if I asked some questions that would assist me to more fully understand the effects of all of this trouble on your lives?' Lucy and Tom gave me the go ahead, and before long I was learning that this trouble had painted a highly negative picture of Lucy's identity as a mother, one that had made it very difficult for her to have connections with other mothers around the subject of parenting. On account of this, it had been quite isolating of her. I also learned that this trouble had negatively affected her relationship with Daniel, blocking what she would otherwise have to give to her son. 'What is it like for you that this trouble has so powerfully influenced your picture of yourself as a mother?', I asked Lucy. And, 'How do you feel about the extent to which all this trouble has come between you and Daniel?' In response to these questions, Lucy became quite tearful. I asked what the tears were all about, and Lucy began to tell me about her deep sadness over what she was missing out on as a mother, and about what she felt cheated of in not knowing her son as she might.

Turning to Tom, I asked about what he would say about the most significant effects of this trouble on his life. He was at first nonplussed by my question. He said that he hardly knew where to start. So I asked him about in which ways this trouble had specifically affected his sense of being Daniel's father. Tom responded that he had never been able to get onto the map in terms of being a father to Daniel – Daniel had never allowed him to assume such a place. 'Is this state of affairs okay with you Tom?', I asked. His response was one of part resignation and part despair: 'Oh, I had my dreams, but what is the point'. I was soon interviewing Tom about these dreams, which we together traced all the way back to the point of Daniel's conception. After a time, I asked: 'So what would you say all of this trouble has done to those dreams'. His emotionally laden response was: 'It has crushed them'.

It was now time to turn to Daniel. 'Would it be okay with you', I asked Tom and Lucy, 'if I now consulted Daniel about the effects of all of this trouble on his life?' 'Go ahead,' Lucy said, 'but I doubt that you will get much out of him'. 'Daniel,' I said, 'As you have heard, I've just been having a talk with your mum and dad about how all of this trouble has been affecting their lives. Now I would like to ask you some similar questions. Would that be okay?' In response, Daniel shrugged his shoulders. I decided to proceed: 'What has this trouble been talking you into about yourself? What sort of picture has it been painting of you?'

Daniel's response to this was to again shrug his shoulders. I said: 'Would it be okay if I was to assume that this shrug meant that it was alright for me to proceed with my questions, and that you will let me know if this isn't the case?' I thought I detected a slight nod. Although I wasn't sure of this, I decided to proceed on this basis of this impression: 'Would it be okay by you if I asked your mum and dad for their thoughts on this?' Another shrug. 'Thanks. I will assume that you are giving me the go ahead, unless you tell me otherwise', I said with some enthusiasm, sensing a degree of collaboration from Daniel.

Upon consulting Lucy and Tom about this question, Lucy said that she thought that this trouble was painting a pretty dismal picture of who Daniel was. Tom elaborated on this, saying that he thought that this trouble was talking Daniel into the idea that he was 'a lazy good for nothing', a 'waste of time as a person', and 'even that he was useless'. These descriptions were the very ones that Tom and Lucy were giving at the outset of our meeting, but they were no longer being collapsed onto Daniel's personhood. These descriptions had been deprived of their authority to characterise Daniel.

What a journey we had been on! At the outset of the interview Tom and Lucy had shared with me a number of highly negative identity conclusions that they and others held about Daniel, and I had suspected that Daniel was secretly in agreement with this appraisal of who he was and of what his life was about – that he believed that these conclusions spoke of the truth of his identity, that he felt at one with these. Now, thirty or forty minutes later, in this conversation, we were experiencing the development of some shared sense that these conclusions didn't speak to the totality of who Daniel was, and that he also had an identity that was somehow separate from, and that even contradicted, these negative conclusions. These negative conclusions no longer represented the truth of who he was.

This opened the door for our work together to become more collaborative. 'Daniel, what is it like for you to be talked into such negative things about yourself?' This time Daniel was shrugless in his response. He glanced at his parents, and, taking this as a cue, I asked them: 'What do you think it is like for Daniel to be talked into such negative ideas about who he is?' In response, Tom said, 'I guess that it makes him lonely – and miserable too'. 'I reckon that he is secretly sad about this', said Lucy, 'because I am sure that the wet patches that I sometimes see on his pillow in the mornings are from tears'. I looked at Daniel, wondering whether or not he would confirm this. Suddenly I saw a tear surfacing in the corner of his eye. We all saw it. Daniel turned his head aside, his tear evaporators working overtime. When he looked back the tear had vanished. But things were never the same after this tear. There was a way forward. The existence of this tear was a signal that Daniel had taken a position on the trouble that everyone else had taken a position on. Now, for what seemed like the first time, there was an opportunity for the members of this family to be joined together, with me, in their efforts to break their lives from what had become such a terrible predicament.

Unpacking negative identity conclusions

Externalising conversations, like the one I have just described, represent just one possibility of many in a range of narrative practices. They are by no means a requirement of narrative therapy and, in fact, externalising conversations are very often absent in my own work with the people who consult me. But they can be very helpful in the unpacking of some of the very negative identity conclusions that people bring with them into therapy.

I am sure that you, the reader, have some familiarity with conclusions of this sort – for example, conclusions that one is 'hopeless', 'a failure', 'incompetent', 'unworthy', 'hateful', 'inadequate', and so on. Perhaps you have had some first-hand experiences of such identity conclusions at some time in your own life, even if this has only been to momentarily entertain a sense of failure to be a real therapist when things haven't been working out quite in the way that you hoped they would! This wouldn't surprise me. After all, the sense of personal failure has never been more freely available to us, and has never been more willingly dispensed as it is in these contemporary times. When these negative identity conclusions are more enduring, people experience them to be quite capturing of their lives. Such conclusions are often found to be paralysing of action in regard to the predicaments of people's lives, and can contribute to a strong sense of one's life being held in suspense, of one's life being frozen in time.

Often when describing and demonstrating the utility of externalising conversations, I have illustrated the extent to which these conversations can contribute to the unpacking of people's negative identity conclusions – which I often refer to as thin conclusions (after Geertz's thin description [1973]). In fact, I believe that one of the primary achievements of externalising conversations is this unpacking of the thin conclusions that people have about their own and about each other's identity. In this activity, these conclusions are deprived of the truth status that has been assigned to them – these conclusions cease to carry the authority that they did. I believe that this outcome is readily apparent in the externalising conversation that I had with Daniel and his parents. Perhaps another brief example will serve to further demonstrate the utility of these conversations in depriving these thin conclusions of their truth status:

Jane was referred to me with a diagnosis of borderline personality disorder. The psychiatry resident, Sarah, who made the referral, was hoping that there was something more that could be done to assist Jane to interrupt the cycle of admissions to hospital. This was a cycle that was fuelled by episodes of cutting, by suicide gestures, and by depression. Early in my conversation with Jane and Sarah, I discovered that Jane believed herself to be a hateful person, and that she hated herself on account of this. In response, and with Jane's permission, I began to interview her and Sarah about the influence of self-hate in her life. This interview was shaped by questions like:

- *What is this self-hate talking you into about yourself?*
- *What seeds is it planting in your mind about who you are?*
- *How does it have you treating your own body?*
- *Does it invite you to nurture your body, or does it require you to reject your body?*
- *Does it have you treating your body with compassion, or does it encourage you to take a hierarchical and disciplinary approach to your body?*
- *What does it want for your connections with other people?*

- *Does this self-hate set itself up as an authority on other people's motives towards you?*

- *How does it do this, and how does this affect your relationships with others?*

- *Would it be okay if I asked some questions to get the low-down on how self-hate speaks, and on the forces that support self-hate?*

These and other questions took us into an extended externalising conversation that had the effect of depriving hatefulness of the truth status it had for so long maintained. This first step in our work together was profoundly significant in its contribution to Jane eventually breaking free of the cycle of hospital admissions, to the discovery of her passion for justice, and to her wider engagement with life.

In summary, in here describing and illustrating the utility of externalising conversations, I have given an account of the extent to which these provide a mechanism for the unpacking of negative and disabling identity conclusions. But this isn't all that I have emphasised when the subject is externalising conversations.

Re-authoring conversations

I have also drawn attention to the part that these externalising conversations play in opening space for yet other conversations, ones that contribute to the generation of more positive identity conclusions. And more than this, these other conversations, that at times I refer to as 're-authoring conversations' (for example, see White, 1992, 1995), also contribute to the identification of and to the exploration of the very knowledges of life and practices of living that are associated with these positive identity conclusions. It is in this way that these re-authoring conversations (that externalising conversations often make way for) contribute to the thick or rich description of people's lives and of their relationships. This thick or rich description of lives and relationships is generative of a wide range of possibilities for action in the world that were not previously visible. It is in these re-authoring conversations that people step into other experiences of their identity. These re-authoring conversations are actually shaping of, or constituting of, life and identity. To illustrate this point, I will return briefly to the story of Daniel.

Our externalising conversation made way for the expression of alternative identity claims on behalf of all family members. These claims contradicted those associated with the problem-saturated story of their lives. These identity claims were implicit in Lucy's distress about what the trouble had been talking her into about herself as a mother, and in her lament about the extent to which trouble was interfering in what she would otherwise have to express in her relationship with Daniel. Alternative claims about who Tom was as a man and a potential father were implicit in his expressions of despair over his crushed dreams. And alternative identity claims about Daniel were present in Lucy and Tom's account of what the trouble had been talking everyone into about his character, and, as well, in his extraordinary tear.

In subsequent conversations, all of the dreams, hopes, purposes, values and commitments that were expressed in these alternative identity claims were drawn out. Amongst other things, the history of Tom's dreams about fatherhood were traced further back to a pledge he had made with himself at the age of fourteen during some very tough times, a pledge that he had never previously spoken of to Lucy or to Daniel. This was a pledge not to do to any future son of his what was being done to him by his own father. Lucy had the opportunity to speak of the connection between the mothering of Daniel and some of the significant purposes and values of her life, and to identify those figures of her history that she was linked to in these. She also provided an account of the initiatives that she had taken in her relationship with Daniel that were a reflection of these purposes and values, which were powerfully acknowledged in the context of our conversations. Daniel, with assistance from Lucy and Tom, began to put words to his tear. These included a previously unacknowledged longing for 'friendship' with his parents and others.

As our conversations evolved, the knowledges of life and practices of living associated with these dreams, pledges, purposes, values and longings were richly described. This provided options for all family members to take initiatives in their relationships with each other, initiatives that hadn't previously been available to them. As an outcome of this, trouble ceased to be a significant presence in the lives of these three people.

In summary, I have emphasised and illustrated the potential of externalising conversations to (a) assist people to break from negative identity conclusions, and to (b) pave the way for the introduction of other conversations which contribute to the exploration of and generation of more positive identity conclusions. These positive identity conclusions are not stand-alone phenomena. They are associated with specific knowledges of life and practices of living. On many occasions, upon initial inquiry, these other knowledges and practices are only evident in very thin traces. However, it is my understanding that these knowledges and practices have the potential to significantly shape other ways of being in the world, and other ways of thinking about life. Therefore, if these knowledges and practices can become more richly described throughout the process of therapeutic conversations, then previously unimagined possibilities for action become available to the people who consult us.

I believe the rich description of these other knowledges and practices to be a vital consideration. For the purposes of emphasising this, I will mention the work that I do with men who are referred to me for perpetrating abuse. Amongst other things, the focus of initial conversations is on opening space for these men to take some preliminary steps in assuming responsibility for the abuses that they have perpetrated, and on the development of some understanding of the short-term and potential long-term effects of these abuses on the lives of others. These initial conversations also focus on the deconstruction of the identity conclusions that shape a sense of male supremacy and entitlement, and on the ways of being in life and thinking about life that are associated with these conclusions. But this is not the end of the story – in fact, it is barely the beginning.

I don't have the assumption that providing these men with an opportunity to challenge these 'truths' about identity, and the ways of being in and thinking about life, that are associated with these truths, is sufficient. I do not hold an assumption that this makes it possible for these men to spontaneously step into more understanding and non-abusive ways of life that are the product of some 'intrinsic' knowledge. Rather, what I understand to be crucially important at this time is to assist these men to engage in extended explorations of other knowledges of life and practices of living that are associated with some of the new identity claims that these men arrive at in these conversations. In this way the particularities of other territories of these men's lives are drawn out, and they finally have another place to stand that is outside of those familiar territories which feature abusive ways of being. I believe that it is only with these more extended explorations of other knowledges and practices of living that a significant and enduring sense of personal responsibility can be embraced.

Naturalistic accounts of life and identity

I hope that I have succeeded in introducing a couple of the key aspects of externalising conversations: how they can assist people to break from negative identity conclusions and how they can open space for further re-authoring conversations which involve the rich description of other knowledges of life and practices of living. I now wish to devote some space to clarifying some misunderstandings which commonly occur in relation to these conversations.

One misunderstanding concerns the idea that the positive identity claims that are richly described in this work are somehow representative of the 'truth' of the identity of the persons concerned – the development of these positive identity claims is regularly taken into modern humanist understandings of life. This misunderstanding persists despite the care that I have taken, in what I have written and taught about narrative practices, to emphasise the historical and cultural basis of all identity claims.

Another misunderstanding concerns the alternative knowledges and practices of living that are identified in re-authoring conversations. These are often taken to be the 'true' knowledges and the 'genuine' or 'authentic' practices of life, that are considered to be 'intrinsic' or 'unconscious' in nature. However, I have never considered this to be the case. Rather, I have always assumed these knowledges and practices, that shape other ways of going about life, to be the products of history and culture. They have been constructed in and developed in the contexts of the many institutions of culture, including the institution of the family – be that family of origin, family of imposition, or family of choice.

It is in the context of these misunderstandings that narrative practices are portrayed as 'libratory' practices that are considered to be freeing of people to live a life that is more accurately a reflection of their 'true nature', of their 'essential humanness', and of their 'authenticity'. I believe that this humanist take on narrative therapy is quite understandable, because, in contemporary western culture, humanist discourses have become pervasive in the shaping of our taken-for-granted understandings of most expressions of life. These understandings provide naturalistic accounts of life and identity. In them, identity is taken to be the product of nature, of human nature; a nature made up of 'essences' or 'elements' that are to be 'found' at the centre of who one is. According to this take on life and identity, the problems that people experience are the outcome of forces that are oppressive of, repressive of, or distorting of the essences or elements of human nature. The solution to people's problems that is proposed by these naturalistic notions is to identify, to challenge, and to throw off these oppressive, repressive and distorting forces so that people might have the opportunity to become more truly who they really are, so that they might be free to live a life that is a more accurate reflection of their human nature. According to this version of things, although people's problems can be understood in historical terms – that problems develop over time in the course of people's lives – the account of the solution is on the outside of history. It is a naturalistic account.

Deconstructing naturalistic accounts of life and identity

Now, what is this thing 'human nature'? One thing that is clear is that it hasn't always existed. Another thing that is clear is that, in the history of the concept of human nature, it has not always been the same thing – what are considered to be the primary essences and elements of human nature change from era to era. Here I will briefly review how human nature has been cast in contemporary western culture. For the purposes of this article, in this review I will restrict my focus to those accounts of human nature that emphasise essences or elements that are considered to be personal properties, and that are routinely referred to as 'resources' and 'strengths'.

If I was to ask you, the readers of this paper, whether or not you possessed any personal properties like strengths and resources, it is my guess that a great many of you would respond in the affirmative: 'Why, of course I have these things'. And if I was to ask you whether these personal properties are relevant to your identity, it is my guess that many of you would again respond in the affirmative: 'Of course. But isn't this true for everyone? These are the building blocks of people's identity'. The existence of these elements or essences of a 'self' that we call strengths and resources is now mostly a taken-for-granted fact. But these essentialist ideas about identity are relatively novel ideas, not just in the history of the world's cultures, but also novel in the history of western culture.

Perhaps some cultural comparison might illustrate this point about the novelty of these ideas in the history of the world's cultures:

I am sitting with a group of elders from several Indigenous Australian communities in the Western Desert area of Australia. I am there with a couple of Aboriginal people with whom I regularly work in partnership, and we are discussing, through an interpreter, an assignment we have been invited to step into by these elders. This assignment has to do with addressing some very significant and pressing predicaments and concerns about developments within their communities, all of which relate to the effects of the invasion and occupation of their country by Europeans over two hundred years ago. In this discussion, I learn about many of the initiatives that have already been taken by these elders to address these predicaments and concerns. They had engaged in these initiatives in circumstances that were highly discouraging them.

I am in awe of these initiatives, and would like to find a way of acknowledging this. My efforts to find ways of acknowledging this awe are shaped by my knowledge of the fact that traditional Aboriginal culture is non-essentialist in its understandings of life and identity. This knowledge is important, for what do you think would be the outcome of me reflecting on what these initiatives said to me about the personal strengths and resources of these elders? Probably, under the circumstances, this would be met with silence in the context of our campfire meeting. However, if there had already been the development of some trust in our connections, I predict that the response of these elders might have been a not-so-polite version of:

> *Why don't you keep that Euro-centred psychological claptrap to yourself? Do you have to colonise our understandings of life as well as everything else? When you understand us in these ways you disrespect our ancestors, who are walking beside us and holding our hands, and who make this work possible. And you are disqualifying the Dreaming.*

So, although I am sure that most of us unquestioningly affirm the presence of these elements or essences and consider them to be universal phenomena, the possession of personal strengths and resources is not a general global phenomenon. The peoples of many other cultures still do not understand their lives in these ways. Apart from this, these essences and elements of human nature haven't been around for all that long even in mainstream western culture.

The possession of personal properties has been a growing general phenomenon of western culture for several centuries, one that received a considerable boost with the development of the modern liberal theory that provides much of the foundation of the western democratic state. Modern liberal theory enshrines the individual's right to the ownership of private property, and to the exclusive use of and disposal of anything that might be gleaned from this property. An individual may cultivate his/her property to improve one's assets, or mine it in order to capitalise on one's resources. Along with the individual's possession of land that was legitimated in modern liberal theory was an associated sense of the individual possession of their own identity as a property. It was understood that the self was a manifestation of an internal property, held by individuals, and that this was what gave individuals the ability to use their external property to improve its assets or to garner its resources. This idea of self as a manifestation of specific properties served to legitimate the individual's possession of the fruits of their labour.

In understanding identity as constituted by properties that are owned by individuals, people came to possess themselves. In this possession of the self, it became possible for one to cultivate one's properties to improve one's assets, to mine one's properties in order to capitalise on one's resources, and so on. These days we experience encouragement from every direction to take possession of ourselves, to engage in the internal farming of our lives through self-cultivation, and to take up internal mining enterprises that have us digging deep to get in touch with our personal resources, and to excavate these resources so that they might be brought to the surface, put into circulation and capitalised on.

I would like to emphasise that in here speaking of the humanist re-interpretation of narrative practices as I have, and of the development of identity as personal property in which can be found elements and essences of a self that are frequently referred to as strengths and resources, it is not my purpose to suggest that these are 'wrong', 'bad' or 'unhelpful' ideas. In speaking of these notions about human nature as I have, it is not my intention to be dishonouring of any ideas held precious by whomever might be reading this article. And in unpacking these humanist understandings in the way that I have, it is not my intention to discredit the many significant achievements of humanism. Further, in speaking of these naturalistic or essentialist understandings of life and identity in the way that I have, I am not suggesting that we can totally free ourselves from, or even that we should attempt to avoid in everyday life, trafficking in these understandings when the cultural context of our lives is contemporary western culture. Rather, it has been my purpose to emphasise the fact that:

a) these essentialist or naturalistic ideas that today shape our taken-for-granted understandings of life and identity came to the centre stage of western culture in relatively recent history,

b) human nature has not always been what it now is considered to be, and whatever it is considered to be is always a product of history and culture,

c) we have not always had identities that are our personal property, nor have we always possessed these essences and elements that are usually referred to as strengths and resources, and that

d) in taking an opportunity to deconstruct these naturalistic accounts of identity and life, we don't have to be so tied to the unquestioned reproduction of them in our lives and in our work with others.

In this article, I have restricted my focus to the deconstruction of naturalistic accounts of identity that are taken to be personal property.

However, because there are so many naturalistic accounts of identity available to us today that we didn't have in recent history, there seems to be unlimited scope for the deconstruction of the 'things' of modern identity, even the things of relationship identity. For example, take 'relationship dynamics'. None of us have had these things for very long. Relationship dynamics are a development of recent history, and they have become increasingly popular over the past three decades. In fact, this is so much the case that there can now be no question about the general success of relationship dynamics. These days more and more people are having them, and I wouldn't be surprised if many of the readers of this paper have experienced the development of these in their own relationships.

However, despite the success of relationship dynamics, we can ask the question: 'Is it a good idea to have relationship dynamics?' In raising this question, I am not suggesting that people didn't used to have troubles in their relationships, and even misery, prior to the onset of relationship dynamics in the 1960s. And I am not taking a general position for or against the construct of relationship dynamics. But in raising this question we have the opportunity to address other questions[2]:

- At what point did these ideas about relationship dynamics come to centre stage in our understandings of relationship?

- What were the historical circumstances that gave rise to these?

- To what use have these ideas been put?

- What did these ideas make possible?

- And what are the limitations and hazards associated with this notion of relationship dynamics?

We could ask the same questions about psychological needs, although they have been around a little longer. We first started having these things in the late 1920s and early 1930s. But it's been in the past four decades that psychological needs have really taken off – the recent historical landscape is dotted with huge outbreaks of these things. These days everybody routinely experiences psychological needs, and understands much of what they do in relation to them.

Limitations and hazards of naturalistic accounts of life and identity

In the following discussion I will draw out what I understand to be some of the limitations and hazards associated with naturalistic accounts of life and identity within the context of therapeutic conversations. But before doing so, I want to acknowledge some of the many valuable contributions of humanism in both the micro- and macro-contexts of life. For example, the idea that one's identity is one's own property, in which can be discovered certain essences or elements of human nature, has been put to work in ways that are challenging of acts of domination and exploitation. For a person to claim to own one's voice can be a powerful strategy in the face of the imposition, by others, of authoritative and negative accounts of one's identity. In this strategy, one truth claim, that is deeply historical and cultural, is employed in acts that are challenging of and refusing of other truth claims that are being imposed by others. And there is a great wealth of examples of the ways in which humanist and liberation philosophies have been put to extraordinary uses within the context of significant social movements.

So then, why, if I can acknowledge many humanist achievements, am I interested in deconstructing popular identity claims that are based on naturalistic accounts of life? This is principally because I believe that in the specific context of therapeutic conversations there are a number of limitations and hazards associated with these naturalistic accounts, and that these invariably outweigh the possibilities associated with these notions. I believe that when alternative identity claims, along with their associated knowledges of life and practices of living, are understood to be representative of people's human nature, options within therapeutic conversations are significantly limited. One foremost concern that I have in regard to this is that if people's preferred identity conclusions are assigned a naturalistic status, and if therapeutic conversations are cast as libratory, this will very significantly reduce the options for therapists to take responsibility for what it is that is being constructed in the name of therapy. And more than this. If the outcome of these conversations is understood to be an expression of human nature or of that which is authentically true about people's lives, it becomes very difficult for therapists to embrace any ethical responsibility for the real effects of their conversations with the people who consult them. Another concern, that I have already addressed in this article, has to do with the extent to which these naturalistic accounts close options for the rich description of the knowledges of life and the skills of living that are associated with the preferred identity conclusions that are generated in therapeutic conversations.

I will here briefly review just some of the other limitations and hazards that I believe naturalistic accounts of life pose in the context of therapeutic conversations:

1. First, in reading human expression as a surface manifestation of certain elements and essences that are of one's own nature, these naturalistic understandings tie us firmly to the reproduction of the cherished 'single-voiced' individualities that are a hallmark of western culture – these are the encapsulated and relatively isolated individualities that I am sure readers will be familiar with. In reproducing these single-voiced individualities, these naturalistic accounts of life and identity can shut the door on opportunities for people to engage with more multi-voiced experiences of identity. These are experiences in which the voices of some of the significant figures of one's life become more present when it comes to matters of one's identity (see White, 1997).

2. Second, these naturalistic accounts of identity construct powerful global or universal norms about life, norms that emphasise notions of 'wholeness', of 'self-possession' and of 'self-containment'. In reproducing these global norms within the context of therapeutic conversations, therapists are implicated as agents in the operations of modern forms of social control. These are forms of social control that are based on the normalising judgement of people's lives. This normalising judgement encourages people to further their efforts in the policing of their own lives in order to close the gap between where they stand in the various continuums of health and development and these culturally constructed norms.

3. Third, these naturalistic accounts of life and identity are intimately related to the modern phenomenon of the production of weaknesses and deficits, and of the disorders and the pathologies. For example,

those discourses that contribute to an understanding of identity by evoking elements and essences of a human nature, like strengths and resources, are at one with the discourses that contribute to an understanding of identity by evoking the idea of weaknesses and deficits – people would not understand their difficulties in life as expressions of weaknesses and deficits if there were no strengths and resources. And therapists would not understand people's expressions in terms of pathologies and disorders if it wasn't for the contrasts provided by naturalistic accounts of life.

4.   Fourth, there is the potential for naturalistic accounts of identity to shape understandings that are marginalising of others: 'We managed to get through what others don't survive on account of our personal strengths and resources'. In marginalising others in this way, these naturalistic accounts obscure the contexts of people's lives, including the politics of their experience. This includes conditions of disadvantage that deprive people of the opportunities and material conditions that would make it possible for them to 'get through'. These naturalistic accounts can also be considered to be marginalising on the basis that they obscure the contribution of the 'other' to whatever it is that is taken to be one's preferred identity conclusions, and to the development of one's knowledges and skills of living.

5.   Fifth, naturalistic accounts of people's significant achievements encourage wonder and can be discouraging of curiosity. In the context of therapeutic conversations, such wonder invariably provides a fullstop to wider explorations, whereas curiosity brings with it opportunities for more extended conversations that contribute to an appreciation of complexity. As well, when wonder shapes a therapist's responses to the preferred developments of people's lives, in efforts to acknowledge these developments s/he is vulnerable to reproducing the modern practices of applause that feature judgement – 'giving affirmations', 'pointing out positives', 'providing reinforcements', and varieties of 'congratulatory responses'. This closes the door on options for practices of acknowledgement that feature significant retellings of the stories

of people's lives, which are much more effective in contributing to the rich description of their identities.

I have here outlined some of the limitations and hazards associated with naturalistic accounts of the significant developments of people's lives. It is my contention that therapeutic conversations shaped by these accounts powerfully restrict what otherwise might be rich conversations – conversations that attend to the multi-faceted and multi-storied character of all expressions of living. In so doing, many of the alternative territories of people's lives are left unexplored.

Unpacking naturalistic accounts of life and identity

If these naturalistic accounts dead end what otherwise might be rich conversations that attend to the multi-faceted character of all expressions of life, what options are available to therapists when presented with such accounts? One option is to initiate conversations that might be unpacking of these accounts. Just as externalising conversations can unpack people's negative truths of identity, identity conclusions that have been assigned a positive truth status can be taken into conversations that are unpacking of them.

Although processes that are unpacking of naturalistic accounts of identity are not dishonouring or diminishing of treasured understandings, this proposal often presents us with a significant personal challenge. The proposal to unpack our own preferred identity claims can be experienced as an invitation to step onto and to disturb hallowed ground, and at times it is refused on this basis. Facing this challenge can be difficult. It is one that we are often inclined to turn away from and to avoid. The desire to stay comfortable with our familiar and taken-for- granted understandings of life and identity is strong, and it often seems an easier option to proceed to unpack other people's identity conclusions when these are not the ones that we personally favour, and to preserve our own favoured notions by refusing to question these, and by refusing to submit these to conversations that are unpacking of them. But I believe that the refusal of this challenge and the maintenance of this personal comfort can be at a considerable cost – it can contribute to a life lived thinly.

In the context of therapeutic conversations, a decision not to introduce the option of unpacking naturalistic accounts of identity can be very significantly limiting. It can shut the door on a range of opportunities for us to engage the people who consult us in conversations that will contribute to the rich description of their lives and identities. This will exclude a range of potentially exciting explorations of other territories of people's lives, joy-filled engagements with new vistas and horizons of identity, and the sort of delight that is the outcome of experiencing the unexpected in therapeutic conversations. For it is in the unpacking of these naturalistic accounts of identity that we find so much more than we could have expected to find. Apart from this consideration I believe that a decision not to explore this option will lead to our own lives and our own work being thinly experienced.

Unpacking resilience

I am now sitting with Helen. Her agenda for our conversation is to explore yet more possibilities for addressing the effects of the abuses she had been subject to in her childhood and as a young woman. She considered that she had already managed, with the help of others, to turn back much of this, but wanted to go yet further in what she referred to as the reclaiming of her life. In the early part of our conversation I asked Helen for her understanding of what it was that had seen her through what she had been put through, and of what it was that had contributed to her success in turning back many of the effects of these abuses in the way that she had. In response, Helen said that she thought it was her 'resilience' that had made it possible for her to achieve this. I inquired about the history of Helen's awareness of this resilience, about the first naming of it for herself, and about what this discovery had meant to her.

Helen's responses to my questions put me in touch with the profound significance that she attributed to the discovery of the resilience that she had possessed and expressed through the history of her life. This constituted a highly valued identity conclusion. However, as I began to reflect on my understanding of the significance of this discovery, she said: 'But resilience is not enough. If it was, it wouldn't be necessary for me to be meeting with you now'. I suggested that further explorations of this resilience might provide her with some more avenues for addressing the effects of the abuses she had been through, and requested Helen's permission to ask some questions about this. Helen said that this would be fine. Here I will give just a small sample of these questions. I did not ask these in a barrage-like fashion. Instead, these questions were shaped by and sensitively attuned to Helen's responses.

The first set of questions encouraged Helen to richly describe the ways of being and thinking that resilience is an emblem for:

* *When this resilience is most present for you, how does it affect what you do?*
* *How does it shape how you are in life?*
* *What does it make possible in your relationships with others?*
* *How does it assist you to go forward in your life?*
* *How does it affect what you are thinking at these times?*

The second set of questions engaged Helen in richly describing her relationship with resilience:

* *Do you know how you have been able to maintain a connection with this resilience through all that you have been through?*
* *Have there been times in your life at which you could have been dispossessed of this connection?*
* *What steps did you take to maintain this connection?*

The third set of questions provided an opportunity for Helen to richly describe what it was that had been sustaining of her resilience:

* *Do you have any thoughts about what it was that was sustaining of this resilience over all these years?*
* *For example, did you bring some hopes to this resilience?*
* *Could you say a little about what sort of hopes were sustaining of this resilience?*
* *Do you know how it was that you were not just resigned to what you had been served up in life?*
* *How did you get introduced to the idea that life could be different for you?*

The fourth set of questions engaged Helen in richly describing her discernment of injustice:

- *At what point did you first become conscious of the fact that what you were being put through was not okay? Do you know how you achieved this consciousness?*
- *What is it that this says about your position on justice and injustice?*
- *Would it be okay for me to ask you some questions about how this position on justice has been expressed in your history?*

In response to these questions, Helen developed a rich description of the social skills and of the very knowledges and practices of life that were associated with this notion of resilience; of the skills or know-how that she had developed and put to work in maintaining her relationship with her resilience; of the hopes that had been sustaining of this resilience, and of how she had been introduced to these hopes; and of her position on justice and of the multiplicity of ways that she had taken this up in her own life and on behalf of others. I will provide here a brief example of just one of the avenues of inquiry that were opened by these questions.

In response to questions about how it was that Helen had been introduced to these hopes that her life might be different, she found herself thinking about her class teacher in her second year at high school – Mrs Murphy. Helen had been going through a particularly hard time, and, on account of this, her attention to school work had been minimal and her concentration in class had been poor. To Helen's surprise, Mrs Murphy hadn't been critical of her over this. Instead, she had been highly considerate and patient, and had been quick to show interest in any constructive contributions from Helen – in fact, Mrs Murphy seemed more interested in these contributions than she was in the performance of the top pupils. As Helen was reflecting on these events of her history, she reached a conclusion that Mrs Murphy must have had suspicions about what she was going through. She also had a stronger realisation about the efforts Mrs Murphy had made to befriend her.

This account of events in Helen's second year of high school opened options for conversations about what it was that Mrs Murphy had appreciated about Helen that others were oblivious to, and about how this recognition and acknowledgement may have contributed to Helen getting through what she had. It also opened options for conversations about what Mrs Murphy's actions reflected about the purposes and values that had been important to her in her career as a teacher, and about whether or not Helen's responses to these actions would have been confirming or disconfirming of these purposes and values. As Helen decided that her responses would have been confirming, I encouraged her to speculate about what it might have been like for Mrs Murphy to experience this from her as a young woman of fourteen years of age. The outcome of this very touching and quite emotional conversation was that Helen was able to bring forth Mrs Murphy's presence in her life at times of duress. At these times she now had options for summoning Mrs Murphy's voice on matters of her identity, and this was effective in displacing the voices of those who had perpetrated abuses on her life. When Helen was ready, we located Mrs Murphy, who had retired from teaching, She remembered Helen and was enthusiastic to meet her again and to join our conversations. These conversations were glorious, but that is another story.

Here, I have introduced some of the categories of questions and a brief account of one of the conversations that contributed to a relatively thoroughgoing unpacking of Helen's resilience. It was through this inquiry and conversations like these that Helen achieved her goal of turning back what she had referred to as the 'remnants' of the effects of the abuses of her life. Helen was right. As she had said: 'Resilience isn't enough'. But resilience unpacked was.

A naturalistic account of resilience as a personal property was not enough, but when resilience was seen as an emblem for a range of alternative identity conclusions as well as knowledges about life and skills of living, when the histories of these were more richly described, and when this inquiry encouraged a significant re-engagement with certain figures of her history, many new options for action became available to Helen. These were options that enabled her to turn back the effects of the abuses of her life.

Finally, I will turn to a story that is illustrative of the possibilities that become available to us, as therapists, in the further development of our practices when we have the opportunity to engage in conversations that are unpacking of naturalistic accounts of our work.

Unpacking intuition

Joe, a therapist from a local agency, decided to consult me for supervision. This decision was made in response to a frustration that he was experiencing in his work. In many of his consultations, things just were not working out in the way that he hoped they would. He wanted to be rid of this sense of frustration, and to have a better time of his work. 'Was this frustration a constant presence?', I asked. 'Mostly,' he said, 'although there have been the occasional times when I have been free of it'. I wanted to know how he would account for these times, but Joe found it difficult to define the particularities of this. Eventually he concluded that at these times things seemed to come together for him in almost a fortuitous way, and, if this related to anything that he was doing, it was probably on those occasions that his 'intuitiveness' was present. I inquired about this sense of being intuitive, and discovered that although Joe experienced this to be a highly-prized quality, it was one that was simply too elusive to be relied upon in his day-to-day work.

I wanted to know how things went in Joe's conversations with people when this intuition was present. I heard that at these times he was able to respond in ways in which people 'felt deeply heard and touched', and that these responses seemed to provide a turning point for the people who were consulting him. This was what Joe wanted to experience more of in his work. I asked him if it would be okay for me to ask some questions about his intuition that might be challenging of this notion, but not disrespectful of it. I made it clear that I understood that intuition was something that he treasured, that he may decide not to risk asking questions of it, and that it would be fine should he decide to leave this untouched. I also said that although these questions of intuition were not necessary in order for us to proceed in our work together, the unpacking of this could well be an option that might provide a solution to the frustration that he was having such a difficult time with.

Joe decided to take a chance on this, and invited me to ask some questions of his intuition. So I asked him to catch me up on the circumstances of a recent consultation in which this intuition was featured. He talked about a family that had been consulting him over recent weeks. I interviewed Joe about his experience of intuition in his work with this family, and about his understanding of the family members' responses to his expressions of this. I also interviewed Joe about the events surrounding these expressions. With this information, we then stepped into a conversation that was unpacking of Joe's intuition. This conversation was initiated by a series of questions. I will provide a sample of these here. I did not ask these questions in a barrage-like fashion. Instead, each question was shaped by and sensitively attuned to Joe's previous response.

The first set of questions encouraged Joe to link his therapeutic responses to the invitations offered, by family members, for him to join with them in particular ways:

- *It is my understanding that you experienced this intuition being available to you at a time that your therapeutic responses were being embraced by the people of this family. What awareness do you have of the invitations that had been offered, by family members, for you to join them, in their lives, in the way that you did?*

- *Do you have a sense of which of these invitations you were being most respectful of in your therapeutic responses?*

- *What was it like for you to be invited into these people's lives in this way?*

The second set of questions encouraged Joe to link his expressions to the cues that family members gave about what sort of therapeutic responses would be significant to them. This set of questions also encouraged Joe to provide an account of the skills that he was engaging with that made it possible for him to attend to these cues in the way that he did:

- *This intuition was present at a time when your responses were particularly significant to family members. Do you have any thoughts about what cues they offered about what sort of responses would be significant to them?*

- *Could you provide me with some understanding of how you have developed a sensitivity to such cues? About how you developed these skills in identifying and responding to cues about what therapeutic responses would be more appropriate?*

- *How was this sensitivity expressed in your therapeutic responses?*

- *What can you tell me about some of the contexts of your own life that have provided fertile ground for the development of this sensitivity?*

The third set of questions contributed to the development, on Joe's behalf, of a consciousness of the extent to which some of his therapeutic responses were particularly relevant to the members of this family because they prioritised an agenda that was of shared significance to them all:

- *Intuition was a feature of your work at a time when the people of this family felt that you were honouring of their agenda for the consultation.*

- *How did you go about recognising and allocating a priority to an agenda that was of shared significance to the different members of this family?*

- *What thoughts do you have about how you and family members contributed to the negotiation of this shared agenda?*

The fourth set of questions drew Joe's attention to the skills expressed in his 'understanding ways of being' with this family, and that shaped his responses in a manner that was experienced as resonant, by family members, in terms of their understandings of life:

- *It is your sense that this intuition was active when family members felt deeply understood by you, and when you were expressing yourself in ways that seemed to fit well with their familiar understandings of life. What are you aware of in the history of your own personal experience, that may have been taken up in your understanding of the experiences of the members of this family?*

- *Can you think of any other contexts of your life in which you might have become acquainted with, and skilled in, the understanding ways that you expressed here?*

- *And how did these experiences contribute to the shaping of your therapeutic responses in ways that fitted with understandings of life that were familiar to members of this family?*

The fifth set of questions focussed on the identification of some of the general skills and knowledges employed by Joe in the fashioning of his therapeutic responses:

- *Your intuition was reflected to you in the fact that your therapeutic responses made a significant difference to this family. Could I ask you some questions that might assist you to provide an account of the skills or the know-how that shaped your responses, that contributed to them making a difference?*

- *Could you provide me with some account of the knowledges of life that were expressed in your responses?*
- *What thoughts do you have about the historical contexts of your life that have provided a basis for the development of these skills and knowledges?*

In response to these and other similar questions, Joe developed a rich description of the skills and knowledges that he was engaging with in his work with this family – skills and knowledges for which intuition was an emblem. And in identifying many of the contexts of his life that provided fertile ground for the generation, acquisition, and refinement of these knowledges and skills, he also had an opportunity for a significant re-engagement with his own history. Through this re-engagement with history, the voices of some of the more influential figures of his life were acknowledged, including that of his maternal grandmother, an extraordinary woman who had been a focal point for the working-class community that he grew up in – she had been an unassuming but strong figure who had always been available to support neighbours and friends through times of trouble and desperation, yet never imposed on their lives. In finding new ways of acknowledging the contribution of these figures to his life and work, the voices of these figures were more present for Joe in his ongoing therapeutic explorations.

In subsequent conversations with Joe, there were yet further opportunities to unpack intuition. Within the context of therapeutic conversations, there are many options available to us to render more visible the contributions of the 'other' to preferred therapeutic developments and to preferred therapist identity conclusions – that is, to render more visible the contributions made to these developments and identity conclusions by the people who consult therapists. In the example given above, these contributions included the family-member initiated cues and the invitations that had been extended to Joe, which had been identified and acknowledged in our earlier conversations. Following this, we had further conversations in which we extended our understandings of the contribution of this family to what it was that Joe had identified as intuition.

Such contributions are invariably significant, yet rarely acknowledged. People who consult therapists often go to some lengths in persevering with their therapists through thick and thin. In these efforts, these people are often very understanding of therapists when they lose the plot, are quick to validate therapists when they are on track, and are encouraging and supportive of those therapist responses that strike a chord for them. As well, many of the conversations had with people touch therapists in ways that are sustaining of them in their own lives and in their work with others. When these contributions can be identified and acknowledged in the course of therapeutic conversations, people become aware of options for furthering their partnerships with the therapists they are consulting. In these circumstances, therapists are less likely to experience a sense of burden, and more likely to find their work invigorating.

With the unpacking of intuition, which was for Joe a preferred identity conclusion, and with the rich description of many of the knowledges and skills that this intuition was an emblem for, the frustration that had been so troublesome to Joe dissipated. What had been relatively intangible – intuition – was now something tangible that could be known in its more intimate particularities. These skills and knowledges were now more available to Joe to reproduce in his work with other people seeking consultation, and he began to have a uniformly better time of this work.

Conclusion

In this paper I have described a number of aspects of narrative practice. In the story of Daniel and his family and of the preliminary steps taken to establish a shared position in relation to trouble, and in the story of Jane breaking from self-hate, I have presented accounts of the ways in which externalising conversations can assist in the unpacking of people's negative identity conclusions. I have also addressed the importance of an appreciation of the fact that the unpacking of these conclusions is not enough. Alternative knowledges of life and practices of living, that in the first place are often only visible as faint traces, must be more richly described in order to create new possibilities for action and life. These other knowledges and practices can be understood in various ways. I have proposed that naturalistic accounts of these knowledges and practices, that interpret these as expressions of essences and elements of a 'human nature', are relatively new understandings of life, and that these are culturally and historically specific understandings. Further, I have suggested that, within the context of therapeutic conversations, these naturalistic accounts bring with them particular hazards and limitations that tend to outweigh the possibilities associated with them.

In the retellings of the story of Helen and of the unpacking of resilience, and the story of Joe and of the unpacking of intuition, I have described some of the options that become available for therapeutic conversations when we move beyond naturalistic accounts and into the realms of history, culture and family. It is through this unpacking of these naturalistic accounts that we come to know the history of alternative knowledges of life and practices of living. It is through this unpacking that we come to know how people's lives are linked to the lives of others around shared themes and values. It is through this unpacking that we can engage with the unexpected. This, I believe, can make all the difference.

Notes

1. All names are pseudonyms.
2. The questions that I provide here are Foucauldian.

References

Geertz, C. (1973). Thick description: Toward an interpretive theory of culture. In C. Geertz, *The interpretation of cultures*. New York, NY: Basic Books.

White, M. (1992). Deconstruction and therapy (pp. 3-30). In D. Epston & M. White, *Experience, contradiction, narrative and imagination*. Adelaide, Australia: Dulwich Centre Publications.

White, M. (1995). *Re-authoring lives: Interviews and essays* (pp. 109-151). Adelaide, Australia: Dulwich Centre Publications.

White, M. (1997). *Narratives of therapists' lives*. Adelaide, Australia: Dulwich Centre Publications.

Fostering collaboration – between parents and children, and between child protection services and families

An interview with Michael White by David Denborough

I imagine most therapists can recall times in their practice when meetings with children/young people and their parents have been filled with expressions of conflict and misunderstanding. Would you be happy to speak about what you try to keep in mind as a therapist in these moments?

I often meet with families where there is conflict between children or adolescents and their parents. This conflict has usually contributed to many misunderstandings, hurt feelings, and negative conclusions about the motives of the other. At times this conflict has escalated to the point that there is a near total breakdown of collaboration between these parties, who have become quite polarised. Families often seek the assistance of therapists at this time. In these circumstances, I am very interested in developing avenues for conversation that can foster collaboration.

When families with children and adolescents seek consultation, very often the problem has been collapsed onto the lives of these young people. In the eyes of the parents, and very often in the eyes of the young person, the problem has become a reflection of the young person's identity. As an outcome of this, parents and young people can be quite conflicted with each other over the problem. In these circumstances, externalised definitions of the problem can be negotiated that open space for a broadening of the conversation.

In the context of an externalising conversation, it can be very helpful to these parents and children to have an opportunity to identify a broad range of consequences of the problem in their lives and in their relationships with each other. In identifying these consequences, parents, as well as young people, have the opportunity to give expression to their experience of their frustrations and disappointments in ways that can significantly diminish the conflict over the problem.

Can you say more about why it's so important for parents, as well as children, to have a chance to speak about the effects that the particular difficulties or conflict is having on their lives?

When people find themselves in conflict that is longstanding, and when people are responding to the longstanding conflicts of others, they are often tempted to totalise one party. When it comes to family conflict it can be children or parents who are totalised. Within families it is more often that children are totalised. Within the culture of psychotherapy it is more often the parents who are totalised, and most commonly the mother. The outcome of this is invariably negative. Usually the child and the parents become more alienated from each other as a result of this, and parents become alienated from the counsellor. In initial externalising conversations, it's very important that the influence of the problem on the lives of the parents is not overlooked. Parents can be highly frustrated and anxious about problems they have experienced with their children, and in this context it can be difficult for them to listen to their children's account of the problem and its effects on their own lives.

Can you say more about how these conversations unfold? It is so easy in these circumstances for conversations to descend into parental complaint and then children's denial and then further complaint, and so on … how can this be avoided?

I am very aware of the responsibility that I have to provide an opportunity for these conversations to go well. There are lots of ways of observing this responsibility. If parents are expressing complaints or criticism in relation to some aspect of their daughter or son's life, one option is to interview them about the absent but implicit that is expressed in these complaints. I might inquire as to what these complaints represent in terms of the concerns that the parents have about aspects of their daughter or son's life, in terms of concerns relating to their own lives, and in terms of their relationships with their son or daughter. These concerns might be linked to certain hopes that seem threatened, to values that are being compromised, to purposes that are being frustrated, to aspirations that are being eroded, to a respect for oneself that is being undermined, and so on.

Talking about concerns, and the foundation of these concerns, as well as complaints, enables different sorts of conversations to unfold. For instance, it becomes possible to ask questions that trace a history of what these concerns are founded on. In these circumstances, parents will have an opportunity to speak about particular experiences within their history that are implicated in the development of these hopes, purposes and values. In this way, the initial criticisms and complaints become more particular and more personal as they are embodied in the parents' experiences. As these criticisms and complaints become more particular and personal in this way, the son or daughter is relieved of some of the negative conclusions that have been constructed about their identity. This also has the effect of opening space for the daughter or son to speak of their own concerns, and of the foundation of these concerns.

When this has been achieved, it is then possible to interview the son or daughter about whether they share any of these concerns that the parents have for them, for their own lives, and for their relationship with their son or daughter. At this time it is usually the case that at least one concern of all those expressed is identified as a shared concern. If any of the parents' concerns are even minimally confirmed by the son or daughter, there is now a degree of shared understanding that can provide a foundation for collaborative inquiry. It becomes possible for family members to talk more about not just this shared concern but also about what it is linked to in a way in which all of this becomes much more richly understood. This invariably provides a platform for collaborative action to address the concern.

But what if the child does not share any of the parents' concerns?

If the son or daughter does not share any of the parents' concerns, this provides an opportunity to ask him or her more about this. S/he can be interviewed about why s/he does not have these concerns about their own life, or about their parents' lives, or about their relationships with their parents.

The son or daughter's response to this inquiry can be taken up into a conversation in which they have an opportunity not only to distinguish their own concerns from the concerns of their parents, but to also give an account of the sort of knowledges of life and skills of living that they are developing that provide them with an assurance they needn't be troubled about the concerns that their parents have for their lives. Action that is being taken by the daughter or son on the basis of these knowledges and skills can then be explored.

I find that when these young people have the opportunity to describe their own concerns, as well as the foundation of these concerns in terms of their own hopes, values, purposes, aspirations, and so on, and when they have the opportunity to give an account of their knowledges of life and skills of living that provide them with some assurance that they needn't be troubled by the concerns that their parents have for their lives, that this mitigates their parents' concerns. Not only do parents get some sense that their son or daughter does have their hand on the rudder in guiding their own life, but that their son or daughter also possesses some knowledges and skills that are available to them in the management of the predicaments of their life.

Another benefit of this inquiry is that young people have the opportunity to more richly describe what they give value to and what they intend for their lives, as well as these knowledges and skills, and this becomes more available to them and influential in the shaping of their own actions.

Alternatively, the daughter or son can be interviewed about their understandings of the effects of their parents' concerns on their relationships with their parents and the consequences of this on their own lives. Questions can be asked about which aspects of these consequences they consider unsatisfactory, about why they consider these consequences unsatisfactory, and about what options are available to them that might diminish or resolve these concerns of the parents. This inquiry can open space for young people to speak of what they give value to and of what they intend for their lives, and of the skills available to them in shaping their relationships with others.

I can imagine that it's important to have these different options in mind as you undertake these conversations!

Yes. It's important to know that, whichever way the conversation turns, there are possible avenues to explore that will contribute to fostering collaboration between family members and between the therapist and the family.

What about circumstances in which young people have complaints about their parents?

In this conversation we've mostly been focusing on complaints and concerns that parents have about their children. But young people also have complaints and concerns about their parents and it is possible to address these by inverting the approach that I've been discussing here.

Are there other particular ways in which collaboration can be fostered in conversations with families with children?

There are many. Perhaps I can mention just one other here. This involves positively implicating parents in the skills and knowledge displayed by their children, and is particularly relevant when parents are feeling inadequate and are seeing themselves as failures in their parental roles.
There is a tradition within the field of psychotherapy of negatively implicating parents in children's lives. In other words, whenever a child displays some action that is deemed undesirable, the parent or care-givers are routinely seen to be implicated in this. This tradition of negatively implicating parents often has negative effects for both parents and children. It can have the effect of dividing the child from the parents, reinforcing a sense of incompetency for parents, and it makes it more difficult for the child to be on reasonable terms with their own history.

As an antidote to this, there are many ways in which parents can be implicated positively in their children's expressions of skills and knowledge of life. This is possible even when there are aspects of the parents' management of child-rearing responsibilities that are potentially or actually traumatising. Of course, if a child is being traumatised by their parents, this must be acknowledged and addressed. This is always given priority. However, efforts to address these potentially or actually negative aspects of the parents' actions can be facilitated through implicating the parents positively in aspects of their children's expressions of life.

Can you say more about this?

In the course of therapeutic conversations, it is possible to identify initiatives of the daughter or son that are expressions of competence. These might be initiatives that are demonstrated during the conversation, or they might be initiatives of recent history, for example in stories of the child's actions that demonstrate particular skills and knowledge. These initiatives can be rendered more significant in therapeutic conversations, and the particular knowledges of life and skills of living that the child has demonstrated can be drawn out.

Having accomplished this, a therapeutic inquiry can then bring significant focus to the parents' contribution to the development of these knowledges of life and skills of living expressed in the daughter or son's initiative. This can be done in a way that doesn't subtract in any way from the child's accomplishment.

Are you saying that, in exploring the social and relational history of children's skills and knowledge, it is often the case that parents are implicated in the development of these skills and knowledge?

Yes. It is possible to engage in conversations that implicate parents positively in relation to their children's development of certain skills and knowledges. By tracing the history of a child's knowledge and skills, the relational, social and cultural richness of their life becomes more visible. This provides new options for the child to be on reasonable terms with their own history and provides for the development of a stronger sense of self. And being implicated in the development of some of the special skills and knowledges expressed by their children provides these parents with a place to stand from which they are able to review and to critique aspects of their care-taking that might contribute to undesirable outcomes for their children and for their relationships with them. This positive implication can free parents from a totalisation of their identity in terms of what has gone wrong in their relationships with their children, which releases them from a 'defended posture'.

I would be very interested to hear about whether you think these sorts of collaborative practices are relevant within child protection investigations, in which workers are trying to respond to possible acts of abuse or neglect ...

This is a big topic! The history of child protection action is not a history of collaboration between state agencies and the families being investigated. When speaking with those who have been principally involved in child protection action, when the circumstances are right and people feel that they can be frank, it is very common to hear expressions of regret, regret about how various situations were managed. This regret is not only expressed in relation to the child protection events of decades past, but also in relation to events of more recent history, of contemporary times. In these conversations, regrets are often expressed by people who have worked in child protection investigation, by those responsible for the formulation of child protection policy, and by those people who have been subject to child protection investigation and action, including most parents and a great many of those young people who have been the focus of such investigation and action.

It is an area that is often seen to be pretty fraught with complexities. Are there ways in which child protection responses could be more collaborative?

In recent times there has been a growing society-wide awareness of the negative consequences of non collaborative child protection action, of child protection action that is not founded upon collaboration between child protection services and the families that are the subject of child protection investigation. On account of this, there have been a number of developments relating to more collaborative approaches to child protection investigation. For example, state agencies in various places have instituted programs for meetings with the families of children who are the focus of child protection investigations with the objective of encouraging parents, and at times siblings, to formulate plans that would ensure the safety of the child. In many instances, these meetings occur prior to the institution of more formal legal procedures, and the intention is for the outcome of these meetings to shape any decisions that are made down the track.

These and other initiatives in more collaborative approaches to child protection investigation and action are significant. However, this is only a beginning, and there is still much to be done. For example, now that these forums for consulting families about the safety of children have been developed, what do we need to put into place so that families are prepared to step into these forums with a voice on matters like safety, and with a voice on options for actions that might not just preserve safety and ensure responsibility, but that also might provide some foundation for the recovery of their relationships with the children who are the focus of child protection investigation, and for the redevelopment of these relationships in which the life-giving aspects of these are elevated?

This is an important question because, in many of these families, the very notion of safety is not a generalised concept, and it is important that there be the opportunity for these families to develop this concept ahead of stepping into these forums that are part of the institutionalisation of collaboration in child protection action and investigation. The same can be said about the concept of responsibility. This is often a very underdeveloped concept, particularly for those parents who perpetrate abuse. This is the case for the concept of responsibility for actions that are abusive or neglectful, for the concept of responsibility for ensuring security and safety for the child, and for the concept of responsibility for actions that might be healing for the child. The further development of these concepts of responsibility is a factor quite critical to the parents' participation in these forums, to them having a voice on safety issues, and to them having a voice on life-giving options in regard to child protection action. This focus on concept development brings to our attention the importance of adequate preparation for parents' participation in these forums that have been instituted to promote collaboration.

There is much to be done in developing approaches to child

protection that are more fully collaborative, in developing approaches that will be effective in addressing the regret that is expressed across the decades of child-protection investigation and action. I believe that the development of these approaches will significantly reduce the potential for regret in the future.

What are some other areas within child protection investigations that could be carried out with a greater sense of collaboration?

There are many of these. I have talked about the critical importance of the development of concepts of responsibility. However, at this present time, in most places, legal processes linked to child protection action are not favourable to this development. In fact, it is usually the case that courts are discouraging of this. In the context of law courts, those who acknowledge responsibility for actions that are abusive or neglectful are punished, and this often includes incarceration. Those who deny this responsibility usually suffer few if any consequences before the law. So there is much rethinking to be done about this aspect of child protection investigation, and I believe that this predicament could be effectively addressed in the context of more truly collaborative partnerships between the courts and child protection agencies.

One of the areas in which there is scope for more collaboration in child protection investigation and action is in the consultation of children, and about the lives of children, who are the focus of these investigations. Usually this consultation is shaped by an agenda to determine the facts of the alleged abuse or neglect that these children have been subject to, to identify the consequences of this abuse and/or neglect and, on occasions, to then provide an opportunity for these children to express their experiences of this abuse and/or neglect in ways that might be healing. Rarely, in my experience, is there a significant focus on investigating the actual responses made by these children to what is perceived to be abusive and/or neglectful.

Do you have any idea as to why these sorts of extended consultations of children are so rare?

There are many normative ideas about childhood, and some of these pose an impediment to the extended consultation of these children in child protection investigation. The evaluation of young people's lives against these normative ideas, many of which are founded upon developmental theories, particularly comes into play when the child's role in the family transgresses a taken-for-granted relationship arrangement; when aspects of the child's role conflict with routine and accepted assumptions about the nature of parent/child and child/sibling relationships. Often it is the young person's performance of aspects of the roles that are assumed to be the usual responsibility and sole province of parenthood that triggers this evaluation. These evaluations are frequently expressed in pathologising diagnoses like: 'This is a parentified child', or in negative and popular conclusions like: 'This child is being robbed of his/her childhood'. Such evaluations are usually associated with the forecast of dire consequences, like: 'The outcome of this will be a condition of arrested development in this child'.

I've met many children who are considered 'parentified' and on every occasion it has been clearly apparent that these children are skilled in the nurturing, care-taking and supervision of others. It has always been possible to play a part in acknowledging and honouring these skills, and for children to take pride in their development of these. And it has also been possible to establish support for these children in the expression of these skills, and by providing them with periods of respite. I have also met many adults who, as children, played parental roles in their families, and who were judged to have arrested development on account of this. These adults have lamented aspects of this role in their childhood, but have also acknowledged the possibilities brought to their lives by the care-taking competencies that were established in their childhood. And few, if any, of these people experienced any acknowledgement of these competencies in childhood, or were supported in their parental role. Just imagine the difference that it makes for children to experience acknowledgement for this in childhood!

What implications does this have in thinking about child protection?

When a primary basis for child protection action is theoretical, as in the case of developmental theory providing the foundation for norms against which the child's life is being measured, it becomes very difficult to engage in the sort of extended consultation of young people, and of the parents and siblings, that will provide an account of the actual responses of these young people to the abuses and or/neglect that they are perceived to be subject to. I don't want to be misunderstood on this, for I am not suggesting that developmental theory is irrelevant, or that children's minds are simply more compact versions of the minds of adults; that a child's consciousness is a mini version of adult consciousness. I will reiterate: to take developmental theory and the norms that it sponsors as a primary basis for the evaluation of the young person in response to concerns about the consequences of what is perceived to be abusive and neglectful, is an impediment to the extended consultation of young people, and of their parents and siblings, about the responses of these young people to this perceived abuse and neglect.

On occasions I have also heard you speak about how you think ideas of eugenics continue to influence child protection work. Can you say something about this here?

Yes, I think this is relevant. It is not only norms sponsored by developmental theory that are an impediment to the extended consultation of young people. There are also norms inspired by a modern-day eugenics agenda.

This implicit eugenics agenda is present in conclusions like: 'This child would be better off in a more normal family'. The evaluation of young people's lives according to the norms inspired by this eugenics agenda is often triggered by the presence of disability in one or both of the young person's parents, but is not restricted to this. Historically, eugenics was a movement that was initiated in England in the late nineteenth century. It was a pseudo-scientific movement that sponsored programs for breeding out the characteristics of human life that were considered undesirable. The eugenics movement reached the pinnacle of its achievement mid-twentieth century, and from then on went into a state of decline, being thoroughly discredited in the later decades of the twentieth century. However, I believe that the shadow of this movement and the sentiments about life associated with it, can still be quite influential in shaping the assessment of the needs of young people who are the focus of child protection investigation and action.

What implications does this have for practitioners?

I think it's important to make visible the impediments to the extended consultation of young people. This includes those practices of evaluation of young people's lives against norms that are sponsored by developmental theory and those that are inspired by an implicit eugenics agenda. These are not the only impediments to this extended consultation, but they seem to me to be high up on the list. Rendering these impediments visible has the effect of opening new avenues of inquiry about young people's experience of what is perceived to be abusive and neglectful. Some of these avenues of inquiry provide rich accounts of young people's responses to their experiences of abuse and neglect.

Why is it significant to inquire about children's responses to their experiences of abuse and neglect?

Although it is invariably the case that children do respond to the traumas they are subject to, rarely do I find that they are familiar with these. In fact, at the outset of my conversations with people who consult me about the consequences of trauma in their lives, it is usually the case that their response to what they were subject to is not available to conscious recall. One outcome of this is that children are constructed as passive recipients of the traumas they have been subject to, and this has a highly negative effect on the development of their sense of personal agency – on the development of a sense of being able to intervene in the shaping of their existence, of a sense of the world being responsive to the fact of their existence. Needless to say, this is highly disabling! It contributes to feelings of impotence, emotional paralysis, of futility, and of personal desolation. Very often, due to the limited nature of inquiry in professional contexts, this can eventuate in a lifestyle that has been characterised as one of 'learned helplessness'.

What is an alternative? When working with children who have experienced significant trauma, how can we orientate ourselves to their memories of trauma?

I have proposed that traumatic memory is invariably a half memory, for it is usually the case that an account of the person's response to the traumas of their history is not present in this memory. It has been erased – perhaps because these responses were ridiculed and diminished, or because these responses were not recognised and confirmed or acknowledged in a way that would contribute to them becoming more familiar to the person, and honoured by them. It is in this sense that I have described the significance of restoring traumatic memory to its fullness through the development of a rich account of how a person responded to the trauma they were subject to. These rich accounts include a broad and solid understanding about the foundations of these responses; that is, a broad and solid understanding of what these responses reflect about what the person has intended for their life, and what these responses reflect about what the person gives value to.

Could these sorts of inquiries take place within child protection work?

In consultations with young people who are the focus of child protection investigation, and with their parents and siblings, I believe it to be of vital importance that these consultations include very significant inquiry into the responses of these young people to what is perceived to be abusive and/or neglectful. Such consultations contribute to the development of a full account of the young person's experiences of trauma, one that will render them far less vulnerable to the diminution of their sense of personal agency. It will provide for them a foundation for the development of a sense of being able to intervene in one's life to shape one's existence, and this will be an antidote to experiences of impotence, emotional paralysis, of futility, and of personal desolation. Secondly, the further development of an account of the child's responses to what is perceived to be abusive or neglectful of them has the potential to significantly influence decisions about child protection action. These responses can be supported and further encouraged, and can form a foundation of safety for the young person.

Can you say more about the sorts of knowledge and skills of children who have endured abuse and neglect?

Many of children's responses to what is perceived to be abusive and/ or neglectful are founded upon specific knowledges and skills. There are many categories of these knowledges and skills. One such category involves knowledges about and skill in relation to the creation of contexts of safety. Another involves knowledge about and skill in the care-taking of others. And so on.

If we create a context in which these skills and knowledges can be acknowledged, what then?

Once these skills and knowledges are drawn out, as well as some of the other knowledges and skills that children are routinely employing in life, it becomes possible to trace the history of the development of these. Very often this includes contributions from parents whose ability to parent is under question. Although this parent may have acted in ways that raise concerns about safety and that have precipitated child protection action, it is usually the case that these actions that have aroused concern do not speak to the totality of the child's experiences of these parents.

When the development of some of the child's knowledges of life and skills of living implicate parents whose actions are being questioned or whose suitability to parent is under question, the rich description of their contribution to these knowledges and skills can have a profound effect in shaping their parenting practices. This positive implication of parents can be taken up in therapeutic conversations that focus on the development and redevelopment of parenting practices that are not neglectful or abusive, and that will augment children's lives.

Of course, having said this, I acknowledge that there are occasions upon which abuse and neglect do represent the totality of a child's experience of a parent.

If these ways of implicating parents in the development of children's skills and knowledges contribute to changing parenting practices, then I can see how these fit within a child protection paradigm. Can I just ask you one more question about the extended consultations of children about their responses to abuse and neglect ... Are these relevant only to older children and young people?

I believe there are options in relation to extended consultations that are relevant to the consultation of both older and younger children from the age of four or five on. There are many ways of facilitating the consultation with young children, including through the use of 'stuffed colleagues'.[1] I will say that I have found the contribution of older siblings to be very helpful in the consultation of young children. In fact, I think there are options for extended consultation of children that are relevant in all contexts of child protection investigation, and that these consultations can have a significant effect on shaping subsequent child protection action. This is even the case in circumstances in which young people are in such peril that immediate and decisive action must be taken to remove them from contexts of abuse and neglect.

Well Michael, we have covered a lot of ground. I've really enjoyed this conversation and look forward to the next one!

Note

[1] 'Stuffed colleagues' refers to the use of stuffed toys!

chapter eight

On ethics and the spiritualities of the surface

An interview with Michael White
by Michael Hoyt & Gene Combs

Michael H: I was very moved by the eloquence of your presentation this afternoon. I thought it was practical love. That's what came to my mind: love in practice.

Michael W: I can relate to descriptions like this, and believe that we need to be reclaiming these sorts of terms in the interpretation of what we are doing – love, passion, compassion, reverence, respect, commitment, and so on. Not because love and passion are enough, but because these terms are emblematic of certain popular discourses; because they are associated with discursive fields that are constituted of alternative rules about what counts as legitimate knowledge, about who is authorised to speak of these knowledges, about how these knowledges might be expressed – including the very manner of speaking of them, about in which contexts these knowledges might be expressed, and so on. And these discursive fields are also constituted of different technologies for the expression of, or for the performance of, these knowledges – different techniques of the self, and different practices of relationship. So, what I am saying is that terms of description like love and passion are emblematic of discourses that can provide a point of entry to alternative modes of life, to specific ways of being and thinking; which will have different real effects on the shape of the therapeutic interaction, different real effects on the lives of the people who consult us, and different real effects on our lives as well.

The rise of the 'therapeutic disciplines' has been associated with extraordinary development in the discourses of science, and, of course, in the modern technologies of relationship. So notions of love and of passion haven't been considered relevant to what we might do in the name of therapy. Because we have become alienated from terms of description such as these, the popular discourses that they are emblematic of have not been all that constitutive of our work; these discourses have not had a significant effect on the shape of mainstream therapeutic practices in recent history.

Michael H: Watching you work, I had the thought that in India people put their hands together and they say *Namaste* – 'I salute the divine in you' – meaning 'What the story on the surface is, I see something holy or special'. If you're a Christian you'd say, 'It's the Christ in you' – although I'm not particularly Christian. Watching you work, I keep seeing over and over in the tapes and the discussion with the audience how you hear the positive. I just want to ask you, how you keep doing that? This has been a very congenial audience, but sometimes the patients are unpleasant, they are challenging, they've done miserable things, they've hurt people, abused people, and yet you're able to treat them with this respect, to kind of separate them from the culture that's been imposed on them. Where does that come from? How can I, how can other people, do more of that? Is there a sort of a key or clue that would help us look at people more that way?

Michael W: These are important questions. You have asked two questions. The first was about the spiritual piece, is that right?

Michael H: Yeah. What I'm getting at is not necessarily that we have to be 'spiritual' or 'religious', but it's looking at people and seeing something in them that's more than the story they're presenting, being able to see the positive underneath all this misery and stuff, seeing there's something good there.

Michael W: The notion of spirituality does interest me. In the histories of the world's cultures there have been many different notions of spirituality. I won't attempt to provide an account of these as I've not had the opportunity to study them, and I don't believe that I have even established an adequate grasp of the dominant notions of spirituality in the recent history of my own culture, or for that matter, in the history of my experience. But I am aware of the extent to which spirituality, in this western culture, has been cast in *immanent forms, ascendant forms,* and in *immanent/ascendant forms.*

Ascendant forms of spirituality are achieved on planes that are imagined at an altitude above everyday life. It is when people succeed in rising to these altitudes that they experience God's blessing, whomever that god might be. It is on these planes that an understanding of what would approximate a direct correspondence between God's word and one's life is attainable; it is on this plane that it becomes possible to achieve a relatively unmediated expression of God's word.

Immanent forms of spirituality are achieved not by locating oneself at some altitude above one's life, but by descending into the caverns that are imagined deep below the surface of one's life. This is a spirituality that is achieved by 'being truly and wholly who one really is', 'by being in touch with one's true nature', by being faithful to the god of self. Much of popular psychology is premised on a version of this notion of an immanent spirituality – to worship a self through being at one with one's 'nature'.

And then there are *immanent/ascendant forms* of spirituality, in which spirituality is achieved by being in touch with or having an experience of a soul or the divine that is deep within oneself and that is manifest through one's relationship with a god who is ascendant.

These and other novel contemporary notions of spirituality are of a non-material form. They propose spiritualities that are relatively intangible, that are split apart from the material world, that manifest themselves on planes that are imagined above or below the surface of life as it is lived. Although I find many of the contemporary immanent/ascendant notions of spirituality to be quite beautiful, and the notion of the soul far more aesthetically pleasing than the notion of the psyche, and although I remain interested in exploring the proposals for life or, if you like, the ethics, that are associated with these notions of spirituality, I am more interested in what might be called the material versions of spirituality. Perhaps we could call these the *spiritualities of the surface.*

The spiritualities of the surface have to do with material existence. These are the spiritualities that can be read in the shape of people's identity projects, in the steps that people take in the knowing formation of the self. This is a form of spirituality that concerns one's personal ethics, that concerns the modes of being and thought that one enters one's life into, that is reflected in the care that one takes to attain success in a style of living. This is a transformative spirituality in that it so often has to do with becoming other than the received version of who one is. This is a form of spirituality that relates not to the non-material, but to the tangible. And I believe that this is the sort of spirituality to which Foucault referred in his work on the ethics of the self (1988a, 1988b).

So, to return to your question. When I talk of spirituality I am not appealing to the divine or the holy. And I am not saluting human nature, whatever that might be, if it does exist at all. The notion of spirituality that I am relating to is one that makes it possible for me to see and to appreciate the visible in people's lives, not the invisible. It is a notion of spirituality that makes it possible for us to appreciate those events of people's lives that just might be, or might provide for, the basis for a knowing formation of the self according to certain ethics. The notion of spirituality that I am relating to is one that assists us to attend to the material options for breaking from many of the received ways of life, to attend to those events of people's lives that provide the basis for the constitution of identities that are other than those which are given. And in this sense it is a spirituality that has to do with relating to one's material options in a way that one becomes more conscious of one's own knowing. I hope that this answer to your question is not too obscure, but this provides some account of what spirituality is about for me.

Michael H: No, your response is not obscure. I get the essence. It is about knowing self-formation.

Michael W: Yes. For me a notion of spirituality would have to be about this. It is about the exploration of the options for living one's life in ways that are other in regard to the received modes of being. It is to do with the problematising of the taken-for-granted, the questioning of the self-evident. At times it is about the refusal of certain forms of individuality, about the knowing transgression of the limits of the 'necessary' ways of being in the world; about the exploration of alternative ways of being, and of the distinct habits of thought and of life associated with these ways of being. In many ways it is about seizing upon indeterminacy, and about the re-invention of who we are. And it is about prioritising the struggle with the moral and ethical questions relating to all of this.

Gene: The thing I'm interested in is how people decide which of those possibilities to privilege, and I think that's one of the places where therapists, whether they want to or not, are given power. To become one who one has not been could go in an infinite number of directions.

Michael W: It could, I agree.

Gene: What can you say about what your experience is, what you're guided by? Which of those directions to privilege?

Michael W: In the work itself, this is achieved by consulting people about the particularities of those alternative ways of being. This is to be in ongoing consultation with people about the real effects of specific ways of being in their relationships with others and on the shape of their lives generally. I don't think the goal is to settle on some specific 'other' way of being in the world, to 'fix' one's life. This work engages people with others in ongoing revisions of their images about who they might be, and about how they might live their lives. And it engages people in an ongoing critique of notions of identity that are based on our culture's many naturalised ideas about this. In fact, this work opens options for people to divest their lives of many of these notions. And in so doing, raises options for people to explore the possibilities for disengaging from the sort of modern practices of self evaluation that have them locating their lives on the continuums of growth and development, of health and normality, of dependence and independence, and so on. These options can also constitute a refusal to engage in those modern acts of self-government that have us living out our lives under the canopy of the bell-shaped curve.

Michael H: So we offer them, 'You know, you don't have to be this way. You could continue in the path you're in, but there are alternatives. Would you like to look at those?' Is that ...

Michael W: Yes. Well I guess so, in a fairly crude way of putting it. I think it is about actually joining with people in the knowing exploration of, and the performance of, options for ways of being in life that might be available to them. It is to engage with people in a choice-making, about these options, that is based on expressions of their lived-experience and on expressions of alternative knowledges of life.

Michael H: When we use invitations or wondering or externalising or any kind of deconstructing[1], it seems to me we're still in some way highlighting certain options or suggesting, 'You may want to consider this' – putting it crudely – and that gets into the power differential. Are we in some way subtly suggesting which alternatives they might take?

Michael W: Of course we are influential, and of course there is a power differential. And it has often been claimed that because of this there can be no way of differentiating between different therapeutic practices on the basis of subjugation; that because of this fact of influence and because of this fact of power, one therapeutic practice cannot be distinguished from another; that there is a certain equity between all therapeutic practices in terms of their real effects. But this blurring of important distinctions around forms and degrees of influence within the therapeutic context is unfortunate. In fact, I believe the blurring of this distinction to be a profoundly conservative act that permits the perpetration of domination in the name of therapy, and excuses those actions that establish therapists as unquestioning accomplices of the status-quo.

It has also been said that because we are of our culture's discourses, and that we cannot think and act outside of them, that we are condemned to reproduce, in therapy, the very relations of power and experiences of self, or subjectivities, that it might be our intent to assist people to challenge. What an extraordinarily reductionist, unitary, global, and monolithic account of culture, of life, we are being encouraged to embrace by this account. What are the real effects of this sort of argument? How does it mask contestation, and undermine struggle? In what ways does it contribute to the further marginalisation of alternative knowledges of ways of being in the world, of alternative subjectivities?

In terms of practice, there is a very significant difference between, on the one hand, delivering interventions that are based on some external formal analysis of a problem, or suggesting to people that they should work on their 'independence' or 'growth' or whatever, and, on the other hand, encouraging people to attend to some events of their lives that that just might be of a more sparkling nature – events that just might happen to contradict those plots of their lives that they find so unrewarding and dead-ended – and to ask them to reflect on what these events might say about other ways of living that might suit them and that might be available to them; to join with people in the exploration of the knowledges and practices of life that might be associated with these alternative plots, to contribute to their exploration of the alternative experiences of the self that might be associated with these knowledges and practices, and to encourage them to take stock of the proposals for action that might be associated with all of this. There is an important distinction to be drawn in regard to these two classes of response.

Aside from such distinctions, we can't pretend that we are not somehow contributing to the process. We can't pretend that we are not influential in the therapeutic interaction. There is no neutral position in which therapists can stand. I can embrace this fact by joining with people to address all of those things that they find traumatising and limiting of their lives. I can respond to what people say about their experiences of subjugation, of discrimination, of marginalisation, of exploitation, of abuse, of domination, of torture, of cruelty and so on. I can join them in action to challenge the power relations and the structures of power that support all of this. And, because the impossibility of neutrality means that I cannot avoid being 'for' something, I take the responsibility to distrust what I am for – that is, my ways of life and my ways of thought – and I can do this in many ways. For example, I can distrust what I am for with regard to the appropriateness of this to the lives of others. I can distrust what I am for in the sense that what I am for has the potential to reproduce the very things that I oppose in my relations with others. I can distrust what I am for to the extent to what I am for has a distinct location in the worlds of gender, class, race, culture, sexual preference, etc. And so on.

I can take responsibility in establishing the sort of structures that contribute to the performance of this distrust. As well, I can find ways of privileging questions in therapy that reflect this distrust over ways of asking questions that would propose my favoured ways of living. I can make it my responsibility to deconstruct my notions of life, to situate these in structures of privilege, in regard to which I can engage in some actions to dismantle.

Michael H: Let me read you a quotation, if I may:

> There is a power differential in the therapy context and it is one that cannot be erased regardless of how committed we are to egalitarian practices. Although there are many steps that we can take to render the therapeutic interaction more egalitarian, if we believe that we can arrive at some point in which we can interact with those people who seek our help in a way that is totally outside of any power relation, then we're treading on dangerous ground. (White, 1994, p. 76)

In addition to reflecting on and asking them to reflect on, how else can we stay aware of the ethics of our influence?

Michael W: I think through a significant confrontation with this fact – that there is a power imbalance. When I propose this confrontation, I am not suggesting that this fact be celebrated, and I am not suggesting that the acknowledgement of this fact as a justification for the use of power by the therapist. And in proposing this confrontation, I am not suggesting that distinctions can't be made in regard to different therapeutic interactions on the basis of the exercise of power and on the basis of subjugation. Instead, I am proposing a confrontation that opens possibilities for us to take steps to expose and to mitigate the toxic effects of this imbalance. I am proposing a confrontation that encourages us to explore the options that might be available to us to challenge the interactional practices and to dismantle the structures that support this power relation.

For example, we can set up the sort of 'bottom-up' accountability structures that I have discussed elsewhere (see White, 1994). We can talk with the people who consult us about the dangers and the possible limitations of that power imbalance, and we can engage them in the interpretation of our conduct with regard to this. But, I have also made the point that it would be dangerous for us to believe that it is possible to establish a therapeutic context that is free of this power relation. This would be dangerous for many reasons. It would make it possible for us to avoid the responsibility of monitoring the real effects of our interactions with people who seek our help. It would make it possible for us to deny the moral and ethical responsibilities that we have to people who seek our help, and that they don't have to us. It would make it possible for us to avoid persisting in the exploration of options for the further dismantling of the structures and the relational practices that constitute this power imbalance.

Michael H: It is through accountability structures that this can be achieved?

Michael W: Well, this is part of accountability. Doing whatever we can to render transparent some of the possible limitations and dangers of that power imbalance, and setting up structures that encourage people to monitor this. In this way we are able to more squarely face the moral and ethical responsibilities that we have in this work. And I would again emphasise that it would be perilous to attempt obscure, to ourselves, the fact of this power imbalance. This would only make it possible for us to neglect the moral and ethical responsibilities that we have to the people who consult us.

Michael H: At the beginning of the conference we were asked how would we know by the end if we 'got it'. I've come during the conference more and more to think of therapy as empowerment through conversation. I just want to ask you to reflect on that. How are you defining therapy these days? Or what's an alternative word?

Michael W: First, I'd like to address your initial comment. This idea of being able to predict where we might be at the end of a process if all goes well is, I believe, a sad idea. It is my view that this is an idea that is informed by the dominant ethic of control of contemporary culture, although I do know that many would debate this point. I figure that conferences probably wouldn't be worth going to if we knew, in advance, where we would be at the end of them. There is a certain pleasure or joy available to us in the knowledge that we can't know where we'll be at the end, in the sense that we can't know beforehand what we will be thinking at the end, in the idea that we can't know what new possibilities for action in the world might be available to us at that time. It seems to me that to engage in prediction about where we might be at the end of a process if all goes well is to obscure, and to close down, options for being somewhere else. And why obscure the options for being somewhere else?

Michael H: It could take away surprise and discovery, couldn't it?

Michael W: If I planned to go to a conference, and if I knew beforehand what I would be thinking at the end, then I wouldn't go. [laughter] It is like that with this work. If I knew where we would be at the end of the session, I don't think I would do this work. And this is also true for the sort of reflecting teamwork[2] that is structured according to the narrative metaphor. If reflecting team members got together and prepared their reflections ahead of their reflections – if their reflection was in fact a performance of previously articulated reflections – then it is more likely that team members will be where they predicted they would be at the end of these reflections, and the more likely it will be that everyone will become quite bored and possibly even comatose – and I have witnessed this sort of outcome. On interviewing therapists about their experience of working in this fashion, I find that it is invariably constitutive of their working lives and relationships in ways that are experienced as undesirable.

However, if team members don't undertake these preparations, if they don't know what they will be thinking about and talking about by the time that they arrive at the end of their reflections, and if the teamwork is structured in a way that facilitates this sort of interaction, then it is more likely that their work together will contribute to the shaping of their own lives and relationships in preferred ways.

Michael H: In Zen they would say you need to keep a 'beginner's mind' (Suzuki, 1970). A fresh look, not having things preconceived.

Michael W: So that's my response to the first part of your question. I think we will experience a better outcome from conferences if they contribute to some steps towards building some foundation for some other possibilities that we might not have predicted beforehand. The second part of your question had to do with how I would define therapy. Well, I define it in different ways on different days.

Michael H: What's today's date?

Gene: The sixteenth.

Michael H: At this point in time, at this moment.

Michael W: At this very moment, just for today, I think it has to do with joining with people around issues that are particularly relevant and pressing to them. It has to do with bringing whatever skills we have available to assist people in their quest to challenge or to break from whatever it is that is that they find pressing. It is our part to work with people to assist them to identify the extent to which they are knowledged in this quest. And, it is to join with people in the exploration of how their knowledges might be expressed in addressing the predicaments that they find themselves in.

In this work, people experience being knowledged, but this is not the starting point. Experiencing this is the outcome of a process that is at once characterised by 'resurrection' and 'generation'. As therapists we play a significant role in setting up the context for this. We assist people to gain access to some of these alternative knowledges of their lives by contributing to the elevation of the sub-stories or sub-plots of their lives, by contributing to the resurrection of some of the knowledges of life that are associated with historical performances of these sub-plots. And we join with people in the generation of knowledges of life through the exploration of the ways of being and thinking that are associated with these sub-plots. I have shared my proposals for this process at some length in a number of publications, and will not reiterate them here. Perhaps it would be sufficient to say here that the sub-plots of people's lives provide a route to the exploration of alternative knowledges of life.

It is our part to assist in the identification of possibilities for action that are informed by these other knowledges of life. It is also our part to encourage people to evaluate the desirability of these other ways of being and thinking, through an investigation of the particularities of the proposals for action that are informed by them, through the exploration of the particularities of a life as it is lived through and constituted by these alternative knowledges.

I don't know if this answer to your question is a particularly good or appropriate answer. And if its not a good answer, its my answer for today at least. Perhaps if we do this interview again tomorrow, I just might be able to answer your question differently at that time. This is my hope.

Gene: I guess I just want to make sure I was tracking what you were saying. So, as a therapist, you're curious about and listening for what are at the moment lesser plots, sub-plots, counterplots, whatever, and kind of sorting through those and exploring some of those with the person and asking them which of those might be interesting to them or useful to them?

Michael W: Yes, I guess so. People are explicitly consulted about these sub-plots of their life. If the therapist's position on these sub-plots is privileged – if the therapist's position is primary – then imposition will be the outcome, and collaboration will be not be achieved. To avoid this imposition, and to establish collaboration, before proceeding we need to know how people judge those developments that might provide a gateway to the identification and exploration of these sub-plots – do they see them as positive or negative developments, or both positive and negative, or neither positive nor negative. And we need to engage people in the naming of these sub-plots of their lives. Apart from this, it is also important that we have some understanding of why it is that people so judge these developments and these sub-plots of their lives. How do these developments fit with their preferred accounts of their purposes and values and so on?

But this is not the whole story. It is never just a matter of determining what developments might be interesting or useful to people. This is not predominantly a cognitive thing. In this work, these sub-plots of people's lives are actually experienced by those who consult us. In the course of the work itself, people live these subplots. Or, if you like, people's lives are embraced by these sub-plots. These sub-plots are not stories about life; they are not maps of the territory of life; they are not reflections of life as it is lived. These sub-plots are structures of life, and in fact become more constitutive of life.

And one further point about what is at work here. There is much that remains to be said about the language of this work, about how it evokes the images of people's lives that it does. Many of the questions that we ask about the developments of people's lives are powerfully evocative of other images of who these people might be, and other versions of their identities. These images reach back into the history of people's lived experience, privileging certain memories, and facilitate the interpretation of many previously neglected aspects of experience. So the language of the work, of the very questions that we ask, is evocative of images which trigger the reliving of experience, and this contributes very significantly to the generation of alternative story lines.

Gene: So the expertise you bring ...

Michael H: Well, Michael made a very good distinction, I thought, in the last presentation between expert knowledge, meaning 'I am the expert here', versus an expert's skills, as I took it, meaning knowing how to ask questions in a way that will let the client experience their local expertise, their local knowledge. I think that is very different from the dominant voice.

Gene: So the knowledge you bring is knowledge about how to evoke in an experiential way these alternative images.

Michael W: Yes. I have often been misrepresented on this point. I have never denied the knowledgeableness of the therapist. And I have never denied the fact of therapist skilfulness. I have, however, challenged the privileging of the therapist's knowledgeableness above the knowledgeableness of people who consult therapists. And I have critiqued the 'expert knowledges'. I have critiqued expert knowledge claims, including those that make possible the imposition of global and unitary accounts of life and the development of formal systems of analysis. I have critiqued the power relations by which these expert knowledges are installed, including those that are essential to the normalising judgement of the subject, that are so effective in the government of people's lives. Throughout this critique, I have supported what is generally referred to as, after Clifford Geertz (1983), the 'interpretive turn'.

Michael H: I had the idea that looking for the sparkling 'moments', looking for the 'unique outcomes', looking for the 'exceptions', in a way what we're trying to do is help the person build a past to support a better future, create some kind of structure under them, 'thickening', I think you were using as a phrase, kind of fleshing it out or filling it in. Do I have that idea right?

Michael W: I'm really interested in the conditions under which people might 'take a leaf out of their alternative books', rather than defining a goal and determining what steps might be necessary to reach that goal. When people get to the point of experiencing the unfolding of preferred developments in the recent history of their lives, they have some sense of where their next step might be placed. Such steps are informed by a developing appreciation of a preferred story line.

Michael H: We're making it up as we go along?

Michael W: Yes, to an extent, yes. I say 'to an extent', because, although there might be certain circumstances under which we might witness what we assume to be clear breaks from the 'known', it is rather difficult to think outside of what we specifically know, and, more generally, rather impossible to think outside of knowledge systems.

In regard to the knowing formation of our lives, it seems that we are, to an extent, dependent upon developing an account of how some of our recent steps fit together with classes of steps that can be read as unfolding in sequences through time according to some theme or perhaps plot. Even upon stepping into unfamiliar territories of identity, coherence appears to be a guiding criterion. And because of this, so is culture and its knowledges of ways of being and thinking in the world.

Michael H: Although sometimes as an alternative to the idea of evolution being a continuous process, I think we're getting now into the idea of evolution not being continuous but being discontinuous, punctuated evolution.[3] Stephen Jay Gould (1980) and William Alvarez talk about how things are steady state, and something extraordinary comes along, like meteorites strike the earth stirring up dust which kills the plant-eating dinosaurs, then that wipes out the meat eaters, and that opens the niche for mammals. There can be a sudden shift or something can be discontinuous. I relate this to page six of *Narrative means to therapeutic ends* (White & Epston, 1990), in that table where you talk about 'before-and-after', 'betwixt-and-between', the whole 'rites of passage' idea[4]. Sometimes we see people who feel prisoners of the path they have been on it so long, and how can they leap off it? So, there's these submerged paths, I take from what you're saying, that remind them of other routes.

Michael W: Yes, there are these sudden shifts, these apparent discontinuities. And at these junctures we can feel quite lost. Perhaps it is useful to think of this experience as a liminal or betwixt-and-between phase, one that is understandably confusing and disorienting. There is always a distance between the point of separation and the point of reincorporation. But the question remains: is it possible to break with something without stepping into other ways of being and thinking that are not in some way continuous with something else? Is it possible to step apart from familiar modes of life and of thought and to step into some cultural vacuum, one that is free of contexts of intelligibility? Historical reflection suggests that there are very few sites of radical discontinuity. But there are always margins of possibility.

Michael H: I see what you are saying. We take something as well as separate from something.

Michael W: Yes. We step into other modes of life and of thought that go before us. But I believe that there are opportunities for us to contribute to the 'drift' of these modes of life and of thought, as we live them, through processes that relate to the negotiation of the different subjectivities or experiences of the self that are associated with these, through interpretation, and through the management of indeterminacy.

Perhaps we could say that within continuity there is discontinuity. And this consideration takes us back to the discussion that preceded these comments. I have a problem with the idea of converting metaphors that come from the non-living world, and from biology for that matter, into the realm of human life, which is the realm of practice and of meaning, and a realm of achievement. I don't believe that this is ever a realm of how things just happen to be. For example, the achievement aspects of this realm can be witnessed in the work that people put into attributing meaning to a whole range of experiences, and the extent to which many of their actions are prefigured on this.

Michael H: Rather than mechanising or animalising or taking us to where we're not.

Michael W: Exactly. And I can't think of one metaphor from the non-living world that I think is appropriate to human life and human organisation, to people who live in culture, who live in language, who participate in making meanings that are constitutive of their lives together. But I don't know if this is relevant to this interview or not.

Michael H: It is now. [laughter]

Michael W: Can I just come back to a point that was made earlier? Gene, around the time that we were talking about the image, you asked me about the nature of this work. What was this question again?

Gene: I was trying to imagine how it is that you conceptualise what it is that you do, what it is that you bring to the therapy situation, and I was also just trying to experience as much as I could for myself what it would be like to be you being a therapist. What am I thinking I should do next? To what am I listening?

Michael H: What is going on in Michael's head when he is working?

Gene: Yeah.

Michael W: 'To what am I listening?' is a good question. And I would say that my listening is informed by some of my preferred metaphors for this work. I particularly relate to poetics. I could read you a piece on poetics by David Malouf, because it fits so well with my conception of this work, and because he says it so much better than I could.

Michael H: Please.

Michael W: [searches in his bag and pulls out a type-written page] This is a piece from a book called *The great world* (Malouf, 1991). This book is substantially about men's experience of Australian men's culture. In it David Malouf talks about how poetry speaks:

> How it spoke up, not always in the plainest terms, since that wasn't always possible, but in precise ones just the same, for what is deeply felt and might otherwise go unrecorded: all of those unique and repeatable events, the little sacraments of daily existence, movements of the heart and invitations of the close but inexpressible grandeur and terror of things, that is our other history, the one that goes on, in a quiet way, under the noise and chatter of events and is the major part of what happens every day in the life of the planet, and has been from the very beginning. To find words for that; to make glow with significance what is usually unseen, and unspoken to: that, when it occurs, is what binds us all, since it speaks immediately out of the centre of each one of us; giving shape to what we too have experienced and did not till then have words for, though as soon as they are spoken we know them as our own.

I so relate to this invocation of the 'little sacraments of daily existence'. The word *sacrament* invokes mystery. And it evokes a sense of the sacred significance of the little events of people's lives – those little events that lie in the shadows of the dominant plots of people's lives, those little events that are so often neglected, but that might come to be regarded with reverence, and at times with awe. These little sacraments are those events that have everything to do with the maintenance of a life, with the continuity of a life, often in the face of circumstances that would otherwise deny this.

These little sacraments of people's lives can be read for what they might tell us all about existence, about the particularities of how we exist. I don't believe that there is such a thing as 'mere existence'. Existing is something that we all do, and have obviously been doing now for many, many years. But it has, in so many ways, had such bad press in recent decades. Why is this the case? Why is it becoming so hard for us to read and to appreciate the little sacraments of daily life? Perhaps this is because these sacraments are on the other side of our culture's ethic of control. Perhaps it is because these little sacraments of daily life don't relate all that well to the accepted goals for life in this culture – like demonstrating 'control over one's life'. And perhaps it is because they don't fit with contemporary definitions of the sort of actions that count as responsible actions. I believe that through the metaphor of poetics it becomes possible for us to challenge the marginalising of existence, and to all play some part in the honouring of the those facts that Malouf refers to as the 'little sacraments of daily existence'.[5]

Gene: When you say 'the little sacraments of daily existence' and you talk about finding the words, I find myself thinking about the close of Ken Gergen's (1994) talk this morning. I don't know that it in any way relates to this. He was talking about inchoate experience, that experience that's not yet quite language and yet that is just before. Does that in any way relate to what you're talking about, sort of the next step of making that, sitting with somebody and then bringing that in a language, bringing that into society?

Michael W: What Malouf is saying about the little facts of daily life fits, I believe, with the notion of the 'spiritualities of the surface' that we have been discussing. But I don't know whether or not what I am saying here has any relation to what Ken Gergen was saying. But it might, and I would like to understand more about what he is proposing before responding to your question.

Michael H: It's the 'poetics of experience' as well as the 'politics of experience'.

Michael W: Yes, it is that as well.

Michael H: I heard Robert Bly, the poet, read a long beautiful evocative poem, and someone stood up in an audience and said, 'Robert, what did it mean?' Bly said, 'If I knew what it meant I would have written an essay, not a poem!' [laughter] I thought what Gergen was getting at was the same that special moment, the sacrament, I think some people call it the spirit of life, when it's *happening* rather than just ... I'll have to ask him.

Michael W: It will be interesting to hear what he says.

Michael H: I once asked Ronnie Laing what he thought of transference. I said, 'What's your definition of it or what do you think of it?' He said, 'Oh, it's post-hypnotic suggestion with amnesia'. [laughter] Post-hypnotic suggestion with amnesia, which I relate to the whole idea of *mystification* (Laing, 1967), that we've been sort of programmed or given this suggestion of how to take things, and we don't even remember that we are given it, so we're kind of locked in. I just wanted to ask if that, from a very different frame, is a way of talking about deconstructing? Does deconstructing get one to the consciousness where you recognise you've been, to use a modern word, programmed?

Michael W: Yes. This is a take on the practices of deconstruction that I can relate to. And I would like here to pick up Laing's contribution to the deconstruction of what we are talking about when we are talking

213

about the phenomenon of transference. The notion of 'post-hypnotic suggestion with amnesia' does bring forth the history of the interactional politics that are generative of this phenomenon, and this encourages us to think of the 'technologies of transference' as technologies of power. And, needless to say, since transference is a phenomenon that is invariably psychologised, to bring forth the technologies of transference does serve to deconstruct this.

But these technologies of transference are not just the historical conditions for the constitution of the transference phenomenon. Transference can also be read as the 'trace' of very present power relations. People experience what they call 'transference' most strongly in hierarchical situations when they are in the junior or subject position, and, of course, ideally, although it does occur in less formal contexts, when they are supine and in a state of vulnerability in relation to another person who is sitting erect, one who is considered an established authority on life, and who denies the subject any information that would situate this authority in his/her lived experience, intentions, or purposes. Here I describe just a few of the conditions and technologies of transference.

Perhaps it would be more appropriate to say that the experience of transference is the trace of power relations that are relatively fixed and approaching a state of domination. So, a strong and ongoing experience of transference can cue people to the fact that they are in a subject position in an inflexible power relationship that could lead to domination. This reading of transference opens possibilities for action that can include a refusal of this power relation.

I don't want to be misrepresented on this point. I'm not saying that there is no such phenomenon as transference. And I do understand that there are those who would justify bringing forth this phenomenon with the idea that this establishes a context for working though issues of personal authority, and so on. But I do think that there is a politics associated with this phenomenon, and would raise questions about the deliberate and not so deliberate reproduction of these politics in the therapeutic context. And I would also want to explore the sort of questions that could contribute to a dismantling of the therapeutic structures that reproduce this phenomenon.

Michael H: How would you describe the ethic of your work?

Michael W: To answer this question, we should talk about what is generally meant by ethics. As Foucault (1988a, 1988b) observed, mostly, these days, when people are talking about ethics they are referring to rules and codes, and no doubt these have a place. But it is unfortunate that, in this modern world, considerations of the rule and the code have mostly overshadowed and even replaced considerations of personal ethics. Something precious is lost when institutional codes and rules for the government of conduct supplant notions of personal ethics. It is in the professional disciplines that we see this taken to its limits, and it is done so in the name of assuring appropriate professional conduct.

Invariably, it is argued that the privileging of matters of rule and code is preventative of the exploitation of people who consult therapists. But I don't believe that the elevation of the rule or code has achieved this anywhere the modern world. In fact, it can be argued that such a reliance on the sort of top-down systems of accountability that are associated with systems of rule and code provide fertile ground for the very perpetuation of such injustices, of such exploitation.

At other times, when people are referring to ethics, they are formulating questions about their existence that are informed by what Foucault refers to as a 'will to truth', and, in this modern world, there has been a fantastic incitement to this will to truth. This is a notion of ethics that gives primary consideration to whatever it might be that is understood to constitute expressions of the truth of 'who we are'. The notions of rule and code are central to this version of ethics as well, as whatever it is that constitutes an expression of the truth of who we are is what is informed by the rules of human nature, however nature might be constructed, and however these rules might be determined.

Modern versions of this centre on notions on the rule of needs: 'How might we keep faith with our deepest needs?'. It is chilling to consider the sorts of actions that can be justified according to modern need discourses. It is not difficult to apprehend the extent to which this will to truth marginalises considerations of personal ethics, and obscures matters of discourse in the constitution of people's lives. And this will to truth is still about the rule of law, only in this case, it is a 'natural law'.

Then there is another style of ethical consideration that has a long history in western culture, one that is referred to at those times when clashes of interest become apparent between people. This is the sort of consideration that makes it possible for people to discern between actions that are informed by selfishness on the one hand, or by altruism on the other. According to this determination, if altruism can be discerned in the actions in question, then such actions are judged to be ethical. Sarah Hoagland (1988) observes that this style of ethical consideration is one that women have principally been subject to, and that it has played a central role in women's subordination. She powerfully deconstructs this consideration in her book *Lesbian ethics*.

And other times the criterion of ethical action is not altruism, but 'responsible behaviour' – people can be considered to be behaving ethically when they are taking responsibility in and for their lives. So often, the version of responsibility that is referred to here is one that is informed by the ethic of control. According to this ethic, responsible action is that version of action that reflects independent and singular action on the world that succeeds in bringing about some goal in the relatively short-term, and when these actions are referenced to some universal notion of the good, or some principle, like 'justice' or 'rights'. To behave ethically is to take action that counts in the sense that it 'measures up'. This notion of responsible action that is informed by the ethic of control is the version that Sharon Welch deconstructs in her book *A feminist wthic of risk* (1990).

Michael H: So, what is your account of the ethic of the work we have been discussing?

Michael W: In different places, including during this interview, I have endeavoured to draw out the version of personal ethics that frames the work that I do. I have talked of the knowing formation of the self. I have talked of a version of responsibility which supports a commitment to identifying and addressing the real effects or the consequences of one's actions in the lives of others. And because this is not something that we can independently determine, either by our own interpretations of our immediate experience, or through recourse to some guiding principle, I have talked of the necessity of accountability. This is a specific notion of accountability, a bottom-up version, rather than a top-down version, and it is a version of accountability that is available in partnership with other people, or groups of people. It is an accountability that is in fact constitutive of our lives, one that brings many possibilities for us to become other who we are.

I have also talked of the principle of transparency. This is a principle that is based on a commitment to the ongoing deconstruction of our own actions, of our taken-for-granted ways of being in this work, of our taken-for-granted ways of thinking about life. This is a principle that requires us to situate our opinions, motives and actions in contexts of our ethnicity, class, gender, race, sexual preference, purposes, commitments, and so on.

I have talked of ways of being in the world that have to do with working with others to establish what we could call the 'foundations of possibility' for their lives and for ours. This is not about acting independently on the world to achieve some predicted goal in a proscribed time, but about working collaboratively in the world in taking steps to prepare the foundations for new possibilities in the time that it takes to do this.

And I have talked about many of the other aspects of this ethic, including the extent to which we can make it our business to develop an attitude of reverence for what Malouf calls the little sacraments of daily existence, and the extent to which we can enter into a commitment to challenge the practices and the structures of domination of our culture.

Michael H: So, this ethic suggests a course of action that is distinct from one that is informed by a traditional goal orientation.

Michael W: Yes. It is on the other side of this. But there are important distinctions to be made here. Not all practices that invoke the notion of goal wittingly or unwittingly reproduce this culture's dominant ethic of control. I doubt that anyone would read the work of Steve de Shazer and Insoo Berg in this way.[6] And I also want to state that this is not an argument for a return to long-term therapy. To the contrary. While the ethic of control structures a context in which there are not many events that really count for all that much, this alternative ethic structures a context in which just so much that couldn't be acknowledged previously can be acknowledged. And, in so doing, it provides for an antidote to despair, for a sense of possibility in regard to one's life going forward, and for a broad range of options for further action.

Michael H: Why do you do therapy? Why do you do this work?

Michael W: This is not a new question. Way back in my social work training, which I began in 1967, we were required to address this question. This was in the heyday of structuralist thought. At that time, in response to such questions, only certain accounts of motive were considered acceptable. These were psychological accounts of motive. Accounts of motive that featured notions of conscious purpose and commitment were not fashionable, and were marginalised. Responses to this question that emphasised a wish to contribute to the lives of others in some way, or that were put in terms of a desire to play some part in addressing the injustices of the world, were considered expressions of naivety. Attempts to stand by such expressions were read as examples of denial, lack of insight, bloody-mindedness, etc. On the other hand, to traffick in psychologised accounts of motive was to display insight, truth-saying, a superior level of consciousness, of maturity, and so on. And invariably, the psychologising of motive translated into the pathologising of motive: 'Which of all of one's neurotic needs was being met in stepping into this profession?,' 'How did this decision relate to unresolved issues in one's family of origin?,' 'Did this decision relate to one's attempts to work through an enmeshed relationship with one's mother?', 'Or did this decision relate to one's attempt to work through a disengaged relationship with one's mother?', and so on. I'm sure that you are familiar with questions of this sort, and that we could easily put a list together.

I always believed that this privileging of psychological accounts of motive to be a profoundly conservative endeavour, one that is counter-inspiration, one that could only contribute significantly to therapist experiences of fatigue and burn-out. For various reasons, I could never be persuaded to step into the pathologising of my motives for my interest in joining this profession, and mostly managed to hold onto what were my favoured notions of conscious purpose and commitment. I have no doubt that over the years that expressions of these notions have been a source of invigoration to me, and in recent years have been encouraging therapists to join together in identifying, articulating and elevating notions of conscious purpose and commitment. To this end I have developed an exercise that you can include along with the publication of this transcript. Readers might be interested in meeting with their peers and working through this together. [The exercise immediately follows this interview.]

Michael H: At the beginning of this conference, they showed a short tape that was made two weeks ago of John Weakland greeting the conference, and John invited us to consider what are the priorities in the field now. What is important and what isn't? I wanted to ask if you had a sense of where we're headed, what you think is important, what we need to be doing more of, what you want to privilege?

Michael W: I never want to make a prediction.

Michael H: Not a prediction of where we're going to wind up, but more a sense of ...

Michael W: What's important for us to be looking at?

Michael H: Yeah.

Michael W: It is necessary for us to be taking more seriously what many have been saying about race, culture, gender, ethnicity, class, age, and so on. For too long have we operated with the idea that the people who seek our help have ethnicity and we don't. [laughter] Not only do we need to join with people in assisting them to locate their experiences in the politics of these contexts, but we are challenged to break from the sort of practices that obscure our own location, and to find ways of engaging with others in reflecting on how this location might be effecting how we interpret our experiences of other people lives, and, of course, how it might be effecting our conduct.

Michael H: I heard Joseph Campbell (1983), when someone asked him his definition of mythology, say it's 'other people's religion', which we kind of dismiss as superstition.

Michael W: Unlike ours. Yeah.

Michael H: Let me read a quotation that gets to something I want to ask. In *Experience, contradiction, narrative and imagination* – a wonderful title as I've come to understand it – you and David Epston (1992, p. 9) comment:

> One of the aspects associated with this work that is of central importance to us is the spirit of adventure. We aim to preserve this spirit and know that if we accomplish this, our work will continue to evolve in ways that are enriching to our lives and to the lives of persons who seek our help.

My question, then, is what's next in your adventure? What's sparking your interest now? I know you began to speak earlier today about some social justice projects.

Michael W: This is a difficult question for me. There are so many things that have my attention at the moment, and they are all things that I want to step more into. Yes, some of these activities do have to do with what are often formally referred to as social justice projects. But this is not a discontinuity. I've always refused the sort of distinctions that put what is commonly referred to as clinical practice in one realm, and community development and social action in another. This is not a distinction that I can relate to. It is a distinction that makes it possible for therapists to treat the therapeutic context as if it is exempt from the relational politics of culture, and to disavow the fact that therapeutic interaction is about action in the world of culture.

Perhaps I can answer your question about 'where to from here' in a different way. I recently saw a movie called *Schindler's List*, and then read a piece about the latter years of Schindler's life. At the time he was living in a bed-sitter somewhere in Southern Germany, I think in Munich. He would frequent the local bars, and on those occasions when he found himself in the company of people of his own generation, he would ask the simple question: 'And what did you do?' – referring, of course, to the Holocaust. Now it was my understanding that this was a genuine question, not a to claim moral superiority. I don't know how many people he found who had answers to this question. I found myself reflecting on this question, and thought it relevant to my life. It is a question that could be asked of me in relation to the many abuses of power and privilege, in relation to the many injustices, that I witness in my immediate world. But if anyone approached to ask this question of me right now, I would request a moratorium on it. I would say, 'Please don't ask me this question yet, it is too soon. I'll keep working on the answer, but please come back later in my life. I hope to have an answer, one that is to my satisfaction, at that time'. And I don't think that it will have to be a big answer, or a grand answer.

Gene: I was just the other day at the Holocaust Museum in Washington. I don't know if you've been there yet, but at the end of the museum you come to a Hall of Remembrance. It's a large open space where there are no flash-cameras or loud noises. And when I got there I sat and found myself making a pledge, to myself or God or whatever … It wasn't even in specific words, but it was a clear pledge or a promise.

Michael H: I know what you mean. Michael, in Australia, what does 'fair dinkum' mean?

Michael W: It means something said that is absolutely true, deeply genuine.

Michael H: Michael, Gene: 'Fair Dinkum!'

Conscious purpose and commitment exercise

Introduction

We have discussed the extent to which the privileging of psychological accounts of motive has marginalised statements of conscious purpose and commitment in this work. We have reviewed the extent to which such statements are pathologised in the culture of psychotherapy, as well as the implications of this in regard to the stories that we have about who we are as therapists. The following exercise will engage you in acts of resistance to this, acts that are associated with the elevation and reclamation of statements of conscious purpose and commitment. I suggest that you invite another person or two to join you in this exploration, for the purposes of sharing your responses to this exercise, or for the purposes of being interviewed about these responses.

1. Talk about any experiences that you have had that relate to the psychologising and the pathologising of your motives for choosing this work, or any reinterpretations of this choice that may have encouraged you to mistrust your statements of conscious purposes or your personal commitment to this work.

2. Review what you can assume to be some of the real effects or consequences, in your work and your life, of this psychologising of your motives, and of this pathologising of your accounts of your conscious purposes and commitments.

3. Identify and retrieve some of your very early statements of conscious purpose that relate to your chosen work, however unsophisticated these might have been, and reflect on what this suggests about what you are committed to this work.

4. Share some information about the significant experiences of your life that have contributed to a further clarification of your conscious purposes and commitments in taking up this work, that have generated realisations about the particular contribution that you have a determination to make during the course of your life.

5. Discuss the experiences that you are having in the course of this exercise – those experiences that are associated with engaging in giving testimony, and in bearing witness, to expressions of conscious purpose, those experiences that are associated with the honouring of statements of commitment.

6. Talk about how the elevation of your notions of conscious purpose and the honouring of your statements of commitment could affect:

   a) your experience of yourself in relation to your work,

   b) your relationship to your own life,

   c) your relationship to your colleagues and to the people who seek your help,

   d) the shape of your work and of your life more generally.

Notes

[1.] As White (1991/1993, p. 34) has written:

   According to my rather loose definition, deconstruction has to do with procedures that subvert taken-for-granted realities and practices: those so-called 'truths' that are split off from the conditions and the context of their production; those disembodied ways of speaking that hide their biases and prejudices; and those familiar practices of self and of relationship that are subjugating of persons' lives. Many of the methods of deconstruction render strange these familiar and everyday taken-for-granted realities and practices by objectifying them.

   He goes on (1991/1993, pp. 35–36) to explain:

   Deconstruction is premised on what is generally referred to as a 'critical constructivist,' or, as I would prefer, a 'constitutionalist' perspective of the world. From this perspective, it is proposed that persons' lives are shaped by the meaning that they ascribe to their experience, by their situation in social structures, and by the language practices and cultural practices of self and of relationship that these lives are recruited into. The narrative metaphor proposes that persons live their lives as stories – that these stories are shaping of life, and that they have real, not imagined, effects – and that these stories provide the structure of life.

[2.] See Andersen (1991) and Friedman (1995).

3. See Rosenbaum, Hoyt & Talmon (1990).

4. Building on the work of van Gennep (1960) and Turner (1969), White & Epston (1990); and Epston & White (1995) suggest that rather than attempting to return a patient in crisis to a 'good enough' status quo, if one thinks of the crisis in terms of a 'rite of passage', then a different construction of the problem is invited; different questions may be asked, and progressive movement is fostered in a different direction. By locating the crisis in relation to a *separation phase*, a liminal or *betwixt-and-between phase*, and a *reincorporation phase*, the person can determine (1) what the crisis might be telling him or her about separating from what was not viable for him or her, (2) what clues the crisis gives about the new statuses and roles that might become available, and (3) how and under what circumstances the new roles and statuses might be realised.

5. Along related lines, Bruner (1986, p. 153) reminds us of James Joyce's phrase 'epiphanies of the ordinary'. Mary Catherine Bateson's (1994, p. 56) comment is also cogent: 'As a society, we have become so addicted to entertainment that we have buried the capacity for awed experience of the ordinary. Perhaps the sense of the sacred is more threatened by learned patterns of boredom than it is by blasphemies'.

6. See Berg (1994), Berg & Miller (1992), Chang & Phillips (1993), de Shazer (1985, 1988, 1991, 1993), and White (1993).

References

Andersen, T. (Ed.) (1991). *The reflecting team: Dialogues and dialogues about the dialogues*. New York, NY: W. W. Norton.

Bateson, M. C. (1994). *Peripheral visions: Learning along the way*. New York, NY: Harper Collins.

Berg, I. K. (1994). *Family based services: A solution-focused approach.* New York, NY: W. W. Norton.

Berg, I. K., & Miller, S. D. (1992). *Working with the problem drinker*. New York, NY: W. W. Norton.

Bruner, J. (1986). *Actual minds, possible worlds*. Cambridge, MA: Harvard University Press.

Campbell, J. (1983). *Myths to live by*. New York, NY: Penguin.

Chang, J., & Phillips, M. (1993). Michael White and Steve de Shazer: New directions in family therapy. In S. G. Gilligan & R. Price (Eds.), *Therapeutic conversations* (pp. 95–111). New York, NY: W. W. Norton.

Combs, G., & Freedman, J. (1990). *Symbol story, and ceremony: Using metaphor in individual and family therapy*. New York, NY: W. W. Norton.

de Shazer, S. (1985). *Keys to solutions in brief therapy*. New York, NY: W. W. Norton.

de Shazer, S. (1988). *Clues: Investigating solutions in brief therapy*. New York, NY: W. W. Norton.

de Shazer, S. (1991). *Putting difference to work*. New York, NY: W. W. Norton.

de Shazer, S. (1993). Commentary: de Shazer and White: Vive la difference. In S. G. Gilligan & R. Price (Eds.), *Therapeutic conversations* (pp. 112–120). New York, NY: W. W. Norton.

Epston, D., & White, M. (1992). *Experience, contradiction, narrative & imagination: Selected papers of David Epston and Michael White, 1989–1991*. Adelaide, Australia: Dulwich Centre Publications.

Epston, D., & White, M. (1995). Termination as a rite of passage: Questioning strategies for a theory of inclusion. In R. A. Neimeyer & M. J. Mahoney (Eds.), *Constructivism in psychotherapy* (pp. 339–354). Washington, DC: American Psychological Association.

Foucault, M. (1988a). The ethic of care for the self as a practice of freedom. In J. Bernauer & D. Rasmussen (Eds.), *The final Foucault*. Cambridge, MA: The MIT Press.

Foucault, M. (1988b). Technologies of the self. In L. Martin, H. Gutman & P. Hutton (Eds.), *Technologies of the self*. Amherst, MA: University of Massachusetts Press.

Freedman, J., & Combs, G. (1996). *Narrative therapy: The social construction of preferred realities*. New York, NY: W. W. Norton.

Friedman, S. (Ed.) (1995). *The reflecting team in action: Collaborative practice in family therapy*. New York, NY: Guilford Press.

Geertz, C. (1983). *Local knowledge*. New York, NY: Basic Books.

Gergen K. (1994). Between alienation and deconstruction: Re-visioning therapeutic communication. Keynote address, *Therapeutic Conversations 2 Conference*. Weston, VA.: Institute for Advanced Clinical Training.

Gould, S. J. (1980). *The panda's thumb: More reflections in natural history*. New York, NY: W. W. Norton.

Hoagland, S. (1988). *Lesbian ethics*. Palo Alto, CA: Institute of Lesbian Studies.

Laing, R. D. (1967). *The politics of experience*. New York, NY: Pantheon.

Malouf, D. (1991). *The great world*. Sydney, Australia: Pan MacMillan.

Rosenbaum, R., Hoyt, M. F., & Talmon, M. (1990). The challenge of single-session therapies: Creating pivotal moments. In R. A. Wells & V. J. Giannetti (Eds.), *Handbook of the brief psychotherapies* (pp. 165–189). New York, NY: Plenum Press. (Reprinted in Hoyt, M. F. [1995], *Brief therapy and managed care: Selected papers* [pp. 105–1391]. San Francisco, CA: Jossey-Bass.)

Suzuki, S. (1970). *Zen mind, beginner's mind.* New York, NY: Weatherhill.

Turner, V. (1969). *The ritual process: Structure and anti-structure.* Ithaca, NY: Cornell University Press.

van Gennep, A. (1960). *The rites of passage.* Chicago, IL: University of Chicago Press.

Welch, S. (1990). *A feminist ethic of risk.* Minneapolis, MN: Fortress Press.

White, M. (1993). Deconstruction and therapy. In S. G. Gilligan & R. Price (Eds), *Therapeutic conversations* (pp. 22–61). New York: W. W. Norton. (Original work published in the *Dulwich Centre Newsletter,* 1991, (3), 1–21. Also reprinted in D. Epston & M. White (1992), *Experience, contradiction, narrative & imagination* (pp. 109–152). Adelaide, Australia: Dulwich Centre Publications.)

White, M. (1993). Commentary. The histories of the present. In S. G. Gilligan & R. Price (Eds.), *Therapeutic conversations* (pp. 121–135). New York, NY: W. W. Norton.

White, M. (1994). A conversation about accountability with Michael White. *Dulwich Centre Newsletter,* (2&3), 68–79. (Reprinted in White, M. [1995], *Re-authoring lives: Interviews & essays.* Adelaide, Australia: Dulwich Centre Publications.)

White, M., & Epston, D. (1990). *Narrative means to therapeutic ends.* New York, NY: W. W. Norton.

Printed in Great Britain
by Amazon

13743893R00133